孫
子
兵
法

Sun Tzu's
The Art of War
Plus
The Art of Politics

"Politics is often like war."

"Politics is often like war. Unfortunately, politicians, the media and the voting public seldom have the same degree of realism and discipline with which professional soldiers fight wars. You can indulge your emotions and base your decisions on wishful thinking in politics, in a way that you are not likely to when your own life is on the line in battle."
Thomans Sowell, February 20, 2014, Townhall.com

"War is the continuation of politics by other means...The political object is the goal, war is the means of reaching it, and the means can never be considered in isolation form their purposes."
Karl von Clausewitz

This book contains the only award-winning translation of Sun Tzu's *The Art of War*

The Art of War Plus
The Ancient Chinese Revealed

Multicultural Nonfiction
Independent Publishers
Book Award
2003 - Winner

Award Recognition for *Art of War* Strategy Books by Gary Gagliardi

The Golden Key to Strategy

Psychology/Self-Help
Ben Franklin
Book Award
2006 - Winner

The Art of War Plus The Art of Marketing

Business
Ben Franklin
Book Award
2004 - Finalist

Making Money by Speaking: The Spokesperson Strategy

Career
Foreword Magazine
Book of the Year
2007 - Finalist

Strategy for Sales Managers

Business
Independent Publishers
Book Award
2006 - Semi-Finalist

The Warrior Class: 306 Lessons in Strategy

Self-Help
Foreword Magazine
Book of the Year
2005 - Finalist

Strategy Against Terror

Philosophy
Foreword Magazine
Book of the Year
2005 - Finalist

The Ancient Bing-fa: Martial Arts Strategy

Sports
Foreword Magazine
Book of the Year
2007 - Finalist

The Art of War Plus Its Amazing Secrets

Multicultural Nonfiction
Independent Publishers
Book Award
2005 - Finalist

The Warrior's Apprentice

Youth Nonfiction
Independent Publishers
Book Award
2006 - Semi-Finalist

Sun Tzu's
THE
ART
OF
WAR
Plus

The Art of Politics
Strategy for Campaigns

by
Gary Gagliardi
Shawn R. Frost

Science of Strategy Institute
Clearbridge Publishing

Published by

Science of Strategy Institute, Clearbridge Publishing

   suntzus.com   scienceofstrategy.org   artofwarpolitics.com

First edition, first printing

Copyright 1999, 2001, 2003, 2004, 2013, 2014 Gary Gagliardi/Shawn R. Frost

ISBN 978-1-929194-72-8 (13-digit) 1-929194-72-2 (10-digit)

Library of Congress Control Number: 2014909813

Manufactured in the United States of America.

Interior and cover graphic design by Dana and Jeff Wincapaw.

Original Chinese calligraphy by Tsai Yung, Green Dragon Arts, www.greendragonarts.com.

Publisher's Cataloging-in-Publication Data

Sun-tzu, 6th cent. B.C.

Political science

   [Sun-tzu ping fa, English]

   The art of war plus the art of politics / Sun Tzu and Gary Gagliardi.

   p. 224 cm. 23

   Includes introduction to basic competitive philosophy of Sun Tzu

   ISBN 978-1-929194-72-8 (13-digit) 1-929194-72-2 (10-digit)

Clearbridge Publishing's books may be purchased for business, for any promotional use, or for special sales. Please contact:

Clearbridge Publishing

PO Box 33772, Seattle, WA 98133

Phone: (206)542-8947 Fax: (206)546-9756

Contents

The Art of War Plus
The Art of Politics

Foreword

Sun Tzu for Politics

The purpose of this book is to introduce those in political campaigns to the strategic principles of Sun Tzu's *The Art of War* and their use in politics. Sun Tzu's strategy consists of more than two hundred general principles. Each principle can be applied to any competitive arena in a systematic way. We call these principles *Sun Tzu's Warrior's Playbook*. This work is meant simply as a basic orientation to this method of competitive thinking. Unlike other books on strategy, this work is not a work about strategic planning. It is a work teaching strategic agility, "strategility" for short, the ability to adapt instantly to changes in the competitive environment. In it we use Sun Tzu's original text as a line-by-line template for applying those principles to working in a campaign.

Competitive Strategy

How does *The Art of War* apply to politics? The Chinese title of this work, *Bing-fa*, means literally "martial arts," but Sun Tzu uses the term more broadly to mean "competitive skills." Unlike other works on military strategy, Sun Tzu designed his book to explain the secrets of competition in the broadest terms possible. The only differences between competition in the political arena and military warfare are the types of tools used and the nature of the battle-ground. The only weapon that this book teaches you to use is the most powerful competitive weapon of all—the human mind.

孫子兵法

To borrow from the German general Carl von Clausewitz, politics is war by other means. In many ways, today's competing political parties in local elections resemble the contesting city-states of Sun Tzu's era—in scale and psychology—much more than our nation-states do.

In Sun Tzu's view, success goes not to the most aggressive but to those who best understand their situation and what their alternatives really are. When you have mastered Sun Tzu's system of strategy, you will be able to almost instantly analyze political situations, spot political opportunities, and make the appropriate decisions.

In our adaptation for politics, the principles of strategy agility are tailored to help you in your role as an organizer, communicator, and persuader. This book addresses a range of challenges, including evaluating your supporters and voters, planning a campaign, adjusting to the local voters' specific needs, diagnosing a voter's behavior, and so on. As a campaigner, you have to face a wide variety of issues, and we try to address a broad spectrum of them .

In this work, we present each stanza of *The Art of War* followed by an adaptation of that stanza to the challenges of political campaigns that converts Sun Tzu's ideas from the military arena into the world of elections as consistently as possible. We start by defining politics as a contest, or, more precisely, a comparison, for the citizen's vote.

Sun Tzu's underlying competitive principles are rich and complex. At our website, SunTzus.com , we explore these principles and their step-by-step application in great detail. As an introduction, this book is more limited. We explore the general relationships among these principles in the Introduction, which follows.

The Art of War Plus The Art of Politics is a different type of book on politics. It addresses decision-making strategy in its most critical form. It won't give you any tricks for making speeches or clever phrases for campaign signs. There are plenty of books that address those techniques. Instead, this book focuses on the core issues of political positioning. It teaches the kind of thinking, planning, and decision-making that it takes to have a successful career in politics.

The book first addresses large-scale issues in politics that other books usually overlook. Do you understand the importance and challenges of a career in politics? Are you committed to it? Are you working with the right party and focusing on the right issues? These topics are addressed in the beginning chapters of the text. You cannot be successful in politics unless you are (or are supporting) the right person running in the right arena for the right reason. As you progress deeper into the book, the text delves into a variety of more specific situations and special conditions that will help you with the specific campaigning process that you might be engaged in.

Competition as Positioning

Why is Sun Tzu's strategy so powerful? Sun Tzu saw that our competitive instincts are all wrong. People think of competition as a threat or a fight. When people are challenged, they react in one of two ways. Sometimes, they run away. Other times, people attack those who threaten them. Psychologists call this the "flight or fight reflex." Sun Tzu taches that seeing competition in terms of threats is foolish.

Sun Tzu teaches that competition is simply a comparison. Competition is unavoidable because everyone is constantly comparing everything. People must compare in order to make choices. This comparison is the basis of all politics.

The true opposite of competition is the absence of choice. If we had no choices, we would have nothing to compare. Competition wouldn't exist. Politics wouldn't exist without a choice among candidates and parties. We must understand how political comparisons affects the choices of our potential supporters, political allies, and voters.

The central challenge of competition for most people is that they do not understand how political comparisons are really made. In many general elections, the political choice is based completely on political party. Because of gerrymandering in many areas, the majority of voters always picks the same party. In these cases, the real election, that is, the real choice, is in the primary, choosing who represents that party in the general election. In most elections with an incumbent, there isn't even a true choice in the primary because most voters always choose the incumbent. In these cases, the best choice for a campaigner in not to run except in open, competitive races.

Sun Tzu provides a system for understanding how people make political decisions, even when most people are not aware of the unconscious comparisons that they are making. Sun Tzu teaches that comparisons are made on the basis of the "positions" that various alternatives hold in our minds. Of course, this idea of positioning is well established in the world of politics, but it is simplified to a choice between left and right. Sun Tzu offers a more comprehensive view, one that allows us to escape simple categories and political boxes.

Because of your campaign's political position on various issues, you have certain unique advantages and disadvantages. Once you understand your position, you can see opportunities that are available to no one else. Instead of fighting people, you position yourself to win their support. Instead of running away from challenges, you seek a position that turns that challenge into an opportunity. Strategic agility, strategility, requires mastering the techniques of advancing positions based on events in the political environment.

Positions in Dynamic Situations

People misunderstand the true nature of success. Success doesn't come from using size, power, or money. It comes from using elements of your position to advance your position, winning the majority in an election.

People think they can win the battle of competitive comparison by tearing down opposing candidates. They fight for position through wars of attrition. This is costly to everyone involved. Instead of fighting, Sun Tzu teaches you how to advance your position so that people cannot fight you—and ideally, over time, want to join you.

In Sun Tzu's view, the secret to warfare is not just winning battles. It is winning them quickly and economically. Victory alone is not enough. Sun Tzu teaches that true success is "making victory pay," that is, making victory profitable and rewarding. You must be wary of costly "victories" that consume your time and energy but fail to bring you long-term success in winning a campaign.

This concept of victory maps extremely well onto any realistic view of politics. Your purpose isn't just to get votes; it is to win and hold an office. It is to win campaigns quickly and effortlessly. You want to win in a way that leaves you ready for the next campaign, not so burned out that you need a vacation.

You will be intrigued by the lessons that emerge when you study the *bing-fa*, that is, "the art of war," when applied to politics.

First, Sun Tzu teaches that having a solid campaign technique is not good enough. You must learn to think competitively. Your potential supporters have many other ways to spend their money. You win political races for one reason: you present decision-makers—volunteers, donors, endorsers—with the best possible alternative for investing their political capital.

Second, an essential ingredient of success is picking the right battleground, or, in our political adaptation, getting involved in the right campaigns in the right areas. As a campaigner, you must focus the political process on your potential supporters' problems that your political position, and only your political position, can properly address.

Third, you must also continually innovate. In Sun Tzu's terms, you must always adapt to the changes that take place on the field of battle. This does not mean that you can abandon proven campaign techniques. You must broaden your standard campaign so that it better fits a wider variety of specific voter issues, especially those affected by a recent change.

Next, you must be opportunistic in leveraging changes in the environment. According to Sun Tzu's teaching, you cannot succeed through your own actions alone. You don't create opportunities. You can defend your existing position from attack, but the competitive environment itself must provide the opportunities for political success.

The secret is what we call strategility, recognizing these opportunities when they present themselves and instantly having the confidence to act on them. Voters will vote—or not vote—as they have voted before unless something changes in the environment to get them to rethink their vote. Because you must leverage change, campaigning often requires watchful patience. At other times, campaigning requires instant action. Sun Tzu argues that opportunities are always abundant, since every problem creates an opportunity. The problem is that opportunities are easily overlooked, difficult to recognize and act upon.

Finally, Sun Tzu's view of competition is knowledge-intensive. He sees victory going to the person who is the most knowledgeable. Sun Tzu's focus on information is so clear that he devotes his final chapter, USING SPIES, to it. In the political version, this chapter is adapted as POLITICAL INTELLIGENCE. In Sun Tzu's system, there is no substitute for good information. Knowledge means having better information than anyone else. For a campaigner, it means knowing more about your area of government and what is really happening than any of your opponents know.

The universal utility of strategy means that you can apply its principles in different ways in different situations. For this reason, you should read and reread Sun Tzu's work over and over, or, better yet, study his competitive key methods more deeply.

With more study, you will develop more insight into Sun Tzu's methods and your own situation. As your situation changes, different parts of the book and different competitive principles will become more important. In general, this book is organized so that the broadest and longest-term issues, such as strategic positioning, are addressed in the initial chapters. Later chapters tend to focus on the special challenges encountered under specific conditions of a campaign. Despite its relatively short length, this book contains more valuable information about good campaign practices than other books two or three times its size. Do not expect to appreciate all of its principles in one reading. Time spent studying Sun Tzu's system of strategility is always time well invested.

Reading this book is simply the first step in mastering the warrior's world of competitive philosophy. As I have said, Sun Tzu's strategic system is sophisticated and deep. Much of its sophistication is not readily apparent simply from reading the text. The Science of Strategy Institute has spent more than a decade detailing the use of Sun Tzu's principles in modern competition. This political adaptation helps you start using Sun Tzu's ideas, but if you are interested in mastering this powerful competitive strategy in politics, it only scratches the surface of what is hidden in the work.

If you want to continue your study of Sun Tzu's principles,

please visit SunTzus.com. Every day on that site, we explain one of Sun Tzu's general principles in detail. Those who become paid members of the Institute get on-line access to our complete *Sun Tzu's Warrior's Playbook*, which explains hundreds of Sun Tzu's principles in terms of simple step-by-step key methods. The Institute also offers a number of audio books, seminars, and on-line training courses in Sun Tzu's methods.

孫子兵法

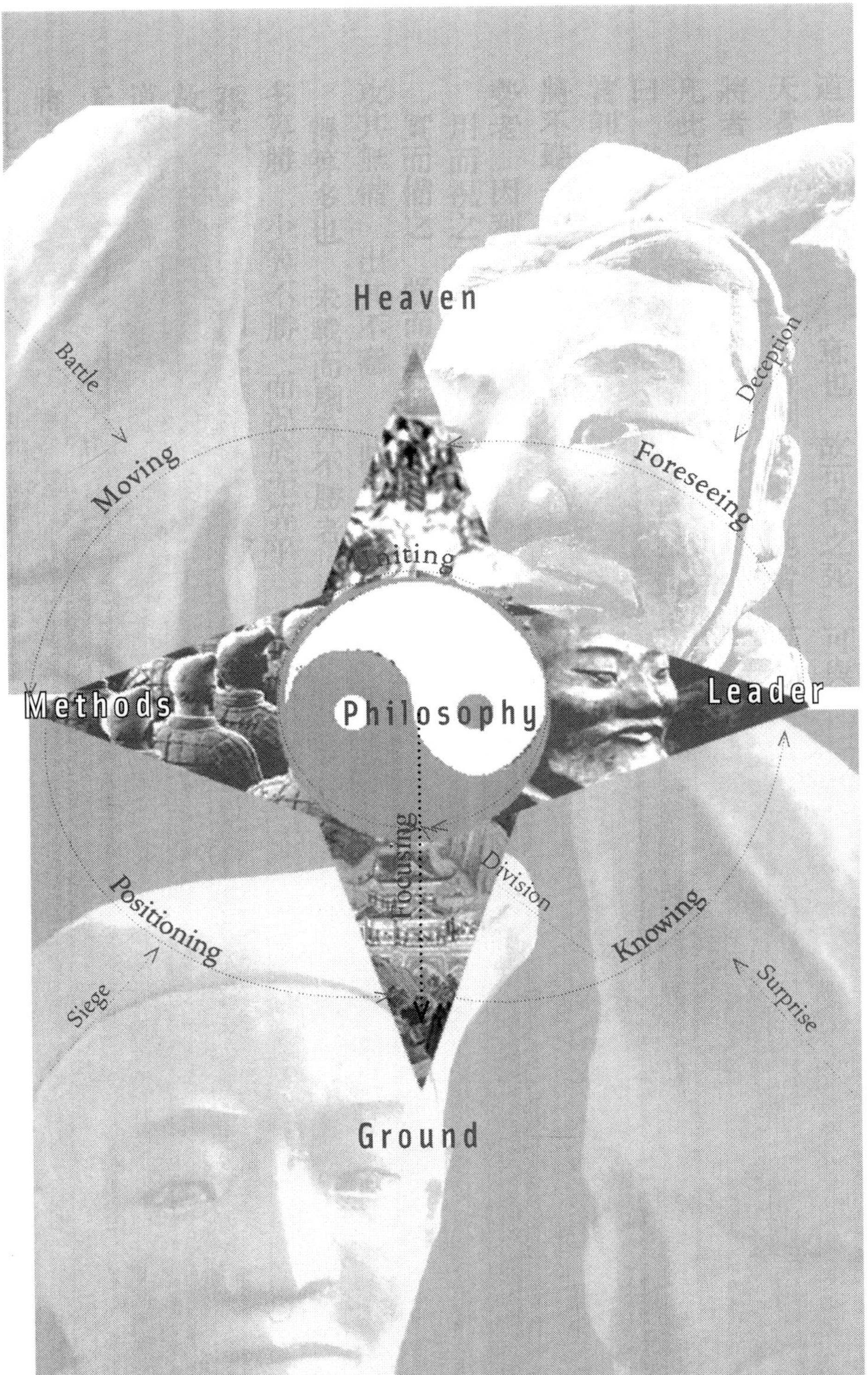
Heaven
Battle
Deception
Moving
Foreseeing
Uniting
Methods
Philosophy
Leader
Focusing
Division
Positioning
Knowing
Siege
Surprise
Ground

Introduction

6.0 Situation Response

5.0 Minimizing Mistakes

7.0 Creating Momentum

4.0 Leveraging Probability

Move

Aim

1.0 Positioning

8.0 Winning Rewards

3.0 Identifying Opportunities

Claim

Listen

9.0 Using Vulnerability

2.0 Developing Perspective

Sun Tzu's Basic Concepts

Sun Tzu wrote his work based on the ancient tradition of Chinese science and philosophy. You will find *The Art of War Plus The Art of Politics* much easier to use if you understand the five elements and the nine skills based upon these ancient traditions.

Sun Tzu saw that success in competitive environments is much more than a matter of winning fights with others. He taught that competition is understood as a comparison between alternatives. Competition occurs whenever a decision or choice between alternatives must be made. Those alternatives are compared and that comparison is the competition. A battle in war is one way comparisons are made between the relative strength of opponents.

However, when battles are avoided, competition also takes place. The comparisons between forces are made in the minds of the generals involved. When one of them decides to avoid the contest, it is because his opponent won that comparison. This is the beginning of strategy, from the Greek word *strategos*, meaning "the thinking of generals."

Many different things are being compared in every type of competition. Sun Tzu described that array of attributes generally as a "position." With this understanding, Sun Tzu realized that the key to success in competition is building and advancing strategic positions. Understanding positions is the first skill that his strategic system teaches. In competitive environments, getting into a winning position is the goal of his system.

Once we understand that competition is a comparison, we realize that its opposite is not cooperation. Competition is necessary for cooperation because a choice must be made between potential partners. The true opposite of competition is "no choice." When we have no choice about our actions, there are no alternatives and no competition among them.

Sun Tzu teaches that a general who fights a hundred battles and wins a hundred battles is not a good general. A good general is one who finds a position that wins without fighting a single battle. You win campaigns by building the political positions and communicating those positions along the paths of least resistance.

Sun Tzu defines the attributes of a position as based on five elements. These five elements—mission, climate, ground, the leader, and methods—define a strategic position and provide the basis for analyzing our positions relative to the positions of others. All the other skills of his toolkit for advancing positions—developing perspective, identifying opportunities, and so on—develop better positions from these elements.

Sun Tzu teaches that every competitor has a unique position within the larger competitive environment. In choosing between your politics and an opponent's, the voter decides based upon your relative positions in this competitive environment. Sun Tzu's system focuses on building up or advancing your position in this environment. Your voters choose the candidates that have what they see as the best position relative to their own.

Sun Tzu teaches that wars of attrition, which are competitive battles in which each competitor tries to tear down the other's position, cannot result in long-term success. This type of competition weakens both contesting parties, opening the way for outside competitors. To avoid wasting resources in such battles, Sun Tzu teaches you how to build positions that competitors cannot easily attack and that supporters want to join.

Sun Tzu's strategy works in competitive environments where outcomes are uncertain. In competitive environments, our decisions collide with the decisions of others, creating conditions that no one planned. In competitive environments, your success depends on constantly adapting to others rather than trying to execute preplanned steps. We call this "strategic agility" rather than "strategic planning." Strategic agility, i.e., strategility, is a method of consistently advancing your position under a wide variety of competitive conditions.

As with so many of Sun Tzu's concepts, this dynamic competitive environment consists of two opposite and yet complementary components, climate (heaven) and ground (earth). Climate and ground describe the key characteristics of time and place within which you compete for votes, that is, the time and geographical region of the election.

Sun Tzu teaches that we view our environment too narrowly. His second key strategic skill defines specific techniques for developing perspective on our position in the environment so that we can see our position as others see us. A political position consists of both an objective reality and a collection of subjective opinions. For example, each candidate's history is an objective reality; however, people's opinions about what that history "means" are subjective. We can change objective reality only by first leveraging subjective opinions.

Climate arises from the forces of change. It is translated as "heaven" or "weather" in Sun Tzu's original text. The cycle of the seasons is the most obvious changes in the natural environment, but every region has its own election cycle and political climate. People's attitudes and emotions are a key component of climate. Sun Tzu's third strategic skill uses change for identifying opportunities in the environment. In the campaigner's environment, economic trends, political issues, and political cycles are used to identify where future opportunities lie.

You and your political party are positioned within a climate of changing political arenas. All issues represent a prediction about what is important for the future. Voters are making decisions today about what will be important in the future. Since they cannot know the future, they make their best guesses about that future. All the emotions involved in the political cycle are based upon fears and uncertainties about what the future will bring.

Ground is the economic foundation of your strategic position. It is both where you fight and what you fight for. As a campaigner, you can think of the ground as your political region, its voters, your supporters, and any alternative candidates. It is the city, county, district, state, or nation that is having the election and the political offices that are being filled. The ground is defined by choices. Candidates choose where to run and the offices for which they run. Voters choose which parties and candidates to support. We must choose the best ground on which to compete in politics. Sun Tzu's fourth strategic skill, leveraging probability, teaches how different types of ground favor some types of positions over others.

Your strategic position is grounded in a specific world (earth) of real voters and their needs. These citizens are your base of financial and volunteer support. Before you battle for votes, you battle with competitors for the limited amount of money and time potential supporters are willing to invest in a given election. Correctly choosing your ground and focusing on winning the best supporters are your basis for political success.

Within the larger competitive environment, your unique characteristics and those of your candidate and your campaign are also part of your strategic position. Sun Tzu breaks the important characteristics of a competitor into two opposite and complementary components: the leader and methods.

A leader is a person who makes decisions in a contest. In a campaign, the key decision-maker might be the candidate, but all those involved, from party leaders to active supporters, are leaders, that is, decision-makers. Leadership is the realm of the individual and subjective opinions. We may act with others, but we must decide for ourselves.

A successful leader must make the right decisions quickly. This demands Sun Tzu's fifth and sixth key skills: minimizing mistakes and situation response. Minimizing mistakes focuses on a necessary economy of action, preserving our limited resources. Situation response teaches us how to choose actions instantly based upon the key conditions that define a situation.

Methods are the techniques of group organization. Our success depends upon working with other people. Methods are the ways in which we interact with others. Standard campaign methods include fund-raising, creating promotional materials, organizing volunteers, and so on. Winning an election requires innovating campaign methods based on existing ones. Sun Tzu's seventh skill is creating momentum, which requires combining standards with innovation. Your job as a campaign leader, as opposed to one of the troops, is to connect the methods of your campaign to advance your political position.

The final element that defines a strategic position is what Sun Tzu calls philosophy and we refer to as mission. A mission defines the goals and values at the core of a strategic position. To create success, this core philosophy must be shared. A clear philosophy and mission unites a political party with its members and gives them focus. A unique philosophy also unites your supporters and your campaign with your voters.

Mission is the basis of rewards. The techniques for winning rewards are the eighth skill in Sun Tzu's system. In politics, this means winning votes and elections. However, it can also mean losing the current election in such as way that you will more certainly win the next. For example, Abraham Lincoln lost every election until he won the presidency. In the end, every decision and action we make in competition must lead to the winning rewards of advancing your position. Sun Tzu's system is economic. You want to use the least time and effort to win the most possible rewards.

A rewarding position consists of the right combination of mission, climate, ground, leadership, and methods. Once we develop a rewarding position, others will try to take it from us. Defending positions is a necessary part of advancing them. It requires Sun Tzu's ninth and final skill, understanding vulnerabilities.

While Sun Tzu's work explains these nine skills for advancing positions, it does not take each skill in turn and explain it in detail. It does not offer examples as a contemporary work might. It does not even offer military examples. It is a work of competitive methods, written about the only weapon that matters in competition, the human mind. It is the human mind that compares positions and makes decisions. This is why Sun Tzu's system works as well in politics today as it has done in military positioning for the past two and a half millennia.

The Art of War was written to be concise. It starts with its most basic concepts, the five key elements, and then addresses progressively more complex and detailed ideas. Along the way, Sun Tzu tries to correct the most common misunderstandings and mistakes that people make in pursuing competitive success. In doing so, he uses analogies, metaphors, and historical references that were familiar to those of his time but are often lost on modern readers. We can adapt these references to the challenges of politics but we cannot capture all of Sun Tzu's meaning.

If you are interested in learning Sun Tzu's principles in more detail, we refer you to our online *Sun Tzu's Warrior's Playbook*. This work details Sun Tzu's nine skills in terms of 232 interwoven principles. Each of these principles is explained as set of step-by-step key methods. Each rule is illustrated by its application to a specific competitive challenge. Many of these challenges are drawn from modern political campaigns.

Chapter 1

Analysis and Your Political Position

Sun Tzu begins his book by giving instructions on how to evaluate strategic positions using five key characteristics.

In the chapter's first part, Sun Tzu describes the five components that define a competitive position—yours, your supporters', your voters', or your opponents'.

In the next section, Sun Tzu describes how to choose an election that you can win.

When you are in politics, it is hard to objectively look at your competitive position, so in the next section he stresses the importance of asking questions and getting outside viewpoints.

Politics is all about voters' perceptions. The discussion in the following section moves to what Sun Tzu calls the use of deception. By "deception" Sun Tzu doesn't mean dishonesty— on the contrary, honesty is one of the necessary characteristics of a leader. His idea of deception equates much more closely to consciously controlling how situations appear to others, the control of perceptions.

The chapter ends with Sun Tzu introducing the idea that strategic analysis demands conscious calculation. The most important choice is the choice of where and when to make a political commitment.

This chapter provides the basic framework of Sun Tzu's strategy, and all these ideas are covered in more detail in later chapters.

Analysis

SUN TZU SAID:

This is war. 1
It is the most important skill in the nation.
It is the basis of life and death.
It is the philosophy of survival or destruction.
You must know it well.

⁶Your skill comes from five factors.
Study these factors when you plan war.
You must insist on knowing your situation.

1. Discuss philosophy.
2. Discuss the climate.
3. Discuss the ground.
4. Discuss leadership.
5. Discuss military methods.

¹⁴It starts with your military philosophy.
Command your people in a way that gives
them a higher shared purpose.
You can lead them to death.
You can lead them to life.
They must never fear danger or dishonesty.

STRATEGY:

Winning is the skill of leveraging positions. Analyze your position by looking at five simple factors.

Your Political Position

THE CAMPAIGNER HEARS:

1 This is politics.
It is the most valuable skill in any nation.
It is the source of a nation's wealth or poverty.
It is a course to success or disaster.
You must study politics seriously.

Using five factors determines your political success.
Consider all these factors when you analyze a given political race.
You use them to know your political position:
1. Talk about your political philosophy.
2. Talk about the changing political trends.
3. Talk about the politics of the geographical area.
4. Talk about each politician's talents.
5. And talk about your campaign process.

MISSION:

Politics begins with a clear set of beliefs.
You must campaign from a position that allows
you to share your voters' goals.
You must help your voters avoid problems.
You must help your voters find success.
Voters must trust your judgment and perspective.

Mission is the core of your politic position. A clear mission creates strength and focus in your position.

*Your position
exists within
a larger com-
petitive environ-
ment, which you
do not control.*

[19]Next, you have the climate.
It can be sunny or overcast.
It can be hot or cold.
It includes the timing of the seasons.

[23]Next is the terrain.
It can be distant or near.
It can be difficult or easy.
It can be open or narrow.
It also determines your life or death.

[28]Next is the commander.
He must be smart, trustworthy, caring, brave, and strict.

[30]Finally, you have your military methods.
They include the shape of your organization.
This comes from your management philosophy.
You must master their use.

[34]All five of these factors are critical.
As a commander, you must pay attention to them.
Understanding them brings victory.
Ignoring them means defeat.

DECISION:

*Good strategic
decisions are
based on seeing
how these five
factors together
create your
position.*

The political climate is how voters feel.
Attitudes change from enthusiastic to negative.
Ideas shift from popular to unpopular.
Climate changes in identifiable patterns.

Your political terrain is the geographic area.
It can be spread out or close by.
It can be resistant or eager to change.
Its voters' minds can be open or closed.
Being in the right political arena determines success or failure.

> **VISION:**
>
> *Your ability to foresee and leverage changes in the environment is the key to your political success.*

Next is your political character.
It must be informed, honest, helpful, fearless, and disciplined.

Finally, you need the right campaign process.
It must fit with existing parties and political groups.
Your campaign process must arise from your political goals.
You must master the best practices.

These same factors are critical to your political success.
You must continuously analyze them.
You must understand them to be successful.
Ignore them and you will fail.

> **LEVERAGE:**
>
> *Your unique opportunities come from your unique position within your political territory.*

You must learn through planning. **2**
You must question the situation.

[3]You must ask:
Which government has the right philosophy?
Which commander has the skill?
Which season and place has the advantage?
Which method of command works?
Which group of forces has the strength?
Which officers and men have the training?
Which rewards and punishments make sense?
This tells when you will win and when you will lose.
Some commanders perform this analysis.
If you use these commanders, you will win.
Keep them.
Some commanders ignore this analysis.
If you use these commanders, you will lose.
Get rid of them.

Plan an advantage by listening. **3**
Adjust to the situations.
Get assistance from the outside.
Influence events.
Then planning can find opportunities and
give you control.

RELATIVITY:

*No position is
good or bad in
itself. You only
understand
positions by
comparing them
to others.*

2 You must pick the right political races.
You must question which campaigns can be won.

In any given campaign, you must ask:
Which party has the preferred philosophy?
Which candidate has the power of incumbency?
Which party does the political climate and geography favor?
What methods of communication influence voters?
Which campaign has the most volunteers and financial support?
Which campaign has the most training and experience?
Is the cost of the campaign justified by the value of an office?
This tells you which campaigns will win and which will lose.
You choose political battles based on this type of analysis.
If you use it, you will be successful.
You will have a successful career in politics.
Too many politicians ignore this analysis.
If you don't analyze positions, most of your campaigns will fail.
Your political career will be short.

3 You discover winnable elections by research.
Campaign for offices you can win.
Use an outside view to see political realities.
Work behind the scenes.
Find campaigns for open seats where your
politics has the advantage.

MYOPIA:

If you fail to get an outside perspective on your political position, you will miss most opportunities.

Warfare is one thing. 4
It is a philosophy of deception.

3When you are ready, you try to appear incapacitated.
When active, you pretend inactivity.
When you are close to the enemy, you appear distant.
When far away, you pretend you are near.

7You can have an advantage and still entice an opponent.
You can be disorganized and still be decisive.
You can be ready and still be preparing.
You can be strong and still avoid battle.
You can be angry and still stop yourself.
You can humble yourself and still be confident.
You can be playing and still be working.
You can be close to an ally and still part ways.
You can attack a place without planning to do so.
You can leave a place without giving away your plan.

17You will find a place where you can win.
You cannot first signal your intentions.

CONTROL:

*Winning begins
and ends with
the power of
information. You
control others by
controlling their
perceptions.*

4 Politics has a single focus.
It is the psychology of using opinions.

If you have a political advantage, seem humble.
When campaigning hard, make it seem effortless.
Where you are similar to opponents, emphasize differences.
When you are very different, emphasize similarities.

When you have a political advantage, invite comparisons.
If you are caught off guard, appear confident.
When you are well prepared, you can still learn more.
When your position is superior, avoid belittling opponents.
When you get upset, stop yourself from showing it.
You can appear modest even when you are confident.
You can have fun even when you are working hard.
You can have political allies and still disagree at times.
You can win on an issue when you didn't expect to do so.
You can give up on an issue without giving up your values.

You will see the right position to win the election.
You cannot be boring and predictable.

REVERSALS:

Emotions are the enemy of campaigning. Whatever you feel, you should show the opposite emotion.

Manage to avoid battle until your organization can
count on certain victory.
You must calculate many advantages.
Before you go to battle, your organization's analysis can indi-
cate that you may not win.
You can count few advantages.
Many advantages add up to victory.
Few advantages add up to defeat.
How can you know your advantages without analyzing them?
We can see where we are by means of our observations.
We can foresee our victory or defeat by planning.

✦ ✦ ✦

PATIENCE:

*Consciously
choosing not
to act is just as
important as
acting decisively
when the time is
right.*

Before investing in a campaign process or a political race, you must know that voters will support your party.

Your voters must have good reasons to vote.

Before wasting your time, you can see when you will not win in a given political environment.

You can find too few reasons for your supporters to vote.

Giving voters good reasons to vote wins political races.

Having too few reasons to vote loses political races.

How can you pick the right elections without analyzing them?

You can see what position will win by what has won in the past.

You can foresee winning or losing an election by analysis.

♦ ♦ ♦

CHOICES:

You advance your position by investing in elections where the five factors are in your favor.

Related Articles from *Sun Tzu's Playbook*

In this first chapter, Sun Tzu introduces the basics of positioning. We explore these ideas in more detail in our Sun Tzu's Warrior's Playbook. *To learn the step-by-step techniques for positioning, we recommend the* Playbook *articles listed below.*

1.0.0 Strategic Positioning: developing relatively superior positions.

1.1.0 Position Paths: the continuity of strategic positions over time.

1.1.1 Position Dynamics: how all current positions evolve over time.

1.1.2 Defending Positions: defending current positions until new positions are established.

1.2 Subobjective Positions: the subjective and objective aspects of a position.

1.2.1 Competitive Landscapes: the arenas in which rivals jockey for position.

1.2.2 Exploiting Exploration: how competitive landscapes are searched and positions identified.

1.2.3 Position Complexity: how positions arise from interactions in complex environments.

1.3 Elemental Analysis: the relevant components of all competitive positions.

1.3.1 Competitive Comparison: competition as the comparison of positions.

1.3.2 Element Scalability: how elements of a position scale up to larger positions.

1.4 The External Environment: external conditions shaping strategic positions.

1.4.1 Climate Shift: forces of environmental change shaping temporary conditions.

1.4.2 Ground Features: the persistent resources that we can control.

1.5 Competing Agents: the key characteristics of competitors.

1.5.1 Command Leadership: individual decision-making.

1.5.2. Group Methods: systems for executing decisions.

1.6 Mission Values: the goals and values needed for motivation.

1.6.1 Shared Mission: finding goals that others can share.

1.6.2 Types of Motivations: hierarchies of motivation that define missions.

1.6.3 Shifting Priorities: how missions change according to temporary conditions.

Chapter 2

Going to War: Choosing a Campaign

To be successful at campaigning, you must understand how to leverage your resources of money from donors and time from volunteers.

Campaigning is expensive. Sun Tzu starts by discussing the economic demands of competition. As a campaigner, you cannot simply spend your way to success. Only by campaigning for offices that are easy to win can you use those resources effectively.

Do not make the mistake of thinking you can spend your way to success. If you want a career in politics, you must avoid a series of losing campaigns. Find races that are easy to win.

If you pick the wrong political races, do not expect support from your political party. Political parties and movements are themselves destroyed by backing the wrong candidates at the wrong time in the wrong regions.

The best way to finance a campaign is to choose to run against weak opponents. If you pick races for open seats and with weak opposing candidates, you can build your campaign by taking away their natural donors and supporters.

Since campaigns demand fund-raising, you must make winning donors a top priority in your campaign. If you pick the right race, finding donors becomes much easier.

In the chapter's final section, Sun Tzu gives the simple key to addressing the financial challenges of politics: winning elections. Holding office addresses the financial issues of politics.

Going to War

SUN TZU SAID:

Everything depends on your use of military philosophy. 1
Moving the army requires thousands of vehicles.
These vehicles must be loaded thousands of times.
The army must carry a huge supply of arms.
You need ten thousand acres of grain.
This results in internal and external shortages.
Any army consumes resources like an invader.
It uses up glue and paint for wood.
It requires armor for its vehicles.
People complain about the waste of a vast
amount of metal.
It will set you back when you attempt to raise
tens of thousands of troops.

ECONOMY:

*Strategy teaches
that the key
to success is
making good
decisions about
using limited
resources.*

12Using a huge army makes war very expensive to win.
Long delays create a dull army and sharp
defeats.
Attacking enemy cities drains your forces.
Long violent campaigns that exhaust the
nation's resources are wrong.

Choosing a Campaign

THE CAMPAIGNER HEARS:

1 Success depends on voters preferring your political philosophy.
All campaigns require contacting large numbers of voters.
Voters must be contacted more than once.
This requires investing in campaign resources.
You need a lot of money and volunteers.
You will always have a shortage of both.
Campaign spending can easily grow out of control.
It uses up resources that people need.
Politicians must defend their spending.
People always complain about the money wasted on politics.
You will not win elections by attempting to spend your way to political success.

Difficult political races are always very expensive to win.
They are a dull waste of time, ending in sound defeat.
Targeting incumbents exhausts your resources.
Long, difficult campaigns that waste your political capital are wrong.

QUICKNESS:

You cannot move quickly if you can only run with a pre-programmed campaign. Flexibility is speed.

AGGRESSION:

Going slowly and "carefully" is more costly and dangerous than moving forward.

[16]Manage a dull army.
You will suffer sharp defeats.
You will drain your forces.
Your money will be used up.
Your rivals will multiply as your army collapses and they will begin against you.
It doesn't matter how smart you are.
You cannot get ahead by taking losses!

[23]You hear of people going to war too quickly.
Still, you won't see a skilled war that lasts a long time.

[25]You can fight a war for a long time or you can make your nation strong.
You can't do both.

Make no assumptions about all the dangers in using **2** military force.
Then you won't make assumptions about the benefits of using arms either.

SMALL IS FAST:

Speed is closely connected to size. Do not mistake costly size for power and safety.

[3]You want to make good use of war.
Do not raise troops repeatedly.
Do not carry too many supplies.
Choose to be useful to your nation.
Feed off the enemy.
Make your army carry only the provisions it needs.

Avoid foolish races.

You will suffer only losses.

They will drain your supporters.

Your donors will be discouraged.

As you lose your political credibility, rivals will be eager to run against you.

It doesn't matter how clever you think you are.

You cannot win elections by wasting resources.

MOMENTUM:

If you are not constantly winning new supporters, you are inviting the loss of your current supporters.

You can join the wrong race too quickly.

But successful political careers rarely start with failure and then endure.

You can run long, drawn out campaigns, or you can have a successful political career.

You can't do both.

2 Make no assumptions about the risks of investing campaign resources.

Then you won't assume the benefits in investing campaign resources.

You want to make good use of your campaign efforts.

Do not keep running in elections you have lost.

Do not accumulate political baggage.

Choose races that are begging for your skills.

Feed off the bad positions of opponents.

Invest only in campaign resources you need.

TESTING:

Each move into a new voter group is a test to see how quickly you can generate support from new voters.

The nation impoverishes itself shipping to troops that **3** are far away.

Distant transportation is costly for hundreds of families.

Buying goods with the army nearby is also expensive.

High prices also exhaust wealth.

If you exhaust your wealth, you then quickly hollow out your military.

Military forces consume a nation's wealth entirely.

War leaves households in the former heart of the nation with nothing.

[8]War destroys hundreds of families.

Out of every ten families, war leaves only seven.

War empties the government's storehouses.

Broken armies will get rid of their horses.

They will throw down their armor, helmets, and arrows.

They will lose their swords and shields.

They will leave their wagons without oxen.

War will consume 60 percent of everything you have.

Because of this, it is the intelligent **4** commander's duty to feed off the enemy.

OPPONENTS:

Strategy demands that you deplete any resources that would naturally go to your competitors.

[2]Use a cup of the enemy's food.

It is worth twenty of your own.

Win a bushel of the enemy's feed.

It is worth twenty of your own.

3 A political movement impoverishes itself investing in races that are out of reach.

Closing a big gap in voter preference is costly for all involved.

Running against any incumbent is also costly.

High costs undermine all campaigns.

If you run in costly elections, you quickly waste limited political resources.

Wasteful campaigns completely destroy political movements.

Failed campaigns leave dedicated political supporters and their party with nothing.

Wasted campaigns destroy would-be politicians.

Seven out of ten campaigns do not make it past the primaries.

Bad campaigns destroy a party's credibility.

Losing political parties lose the support of donors.

They give up protecting incumbents and attacking opponents.

They will lose the best candidates and the safest offices.

They will leave their political supporters without choices.

Poorly run campaigns will shrink the voting base.

4 In all elections, the wise campaigner must feed off weak opponents.

Win donors that give to an opponent.

This is worth twenty times your own money.

Get endorsed by opponents' supporters.

They are worth twenty times expected support.

RESULTS:

Choose target voters from whom you can quickly generate the endorsement to win more supporters.

⁶You can kill the enemy and frustrate him as well.
Take the enemy's strength from him by stealing away his
money.

⁸Fight for the enemy's supply wagons.
Capture his supplies by using overwhelming force.
Reward the first who capture them.
Then change their banners and flags.
Mix them in with your own wagons to increase your supply
line.
Keep your soldiers strong by providing for them.
This is what it means to beat the enemy while you grow
more powerful.

Make victory in war pay for itself. 5
Avoid expensive, long campaigns.
The military commander's knowledge is the key.
It determines whether the civilian officials can
govern.
It determines whether the nation's households
are peaceful or a danger to the state.

♦ ♦ ♦

MAKE IT PAY:

*Success is
defined only by
its profitability.
No victory is
complete until it
returns a benefit
worth the cost.*

You can embarrass opponents and discourage them as well.
Take away your competors' strength by stealing their supporters and donors.

Fight only for competitors' most reliable donors.
Win these donors by focusing on them personally.
Generously reward fund-raisers who win major donations.
Promote every switch in political allegiance.
Mix new sources of support with existing ones to increase your resources.
Keep your supporters happy by winning more resources.
This is what it means to weaken opposition while building your campaign.

5 Winning elections makes fund-raising easy.
Avoid a series of costly losses.
Choosing the right opponents is the key.
It determines whether your political party will support you.
It determines whether your party's local organization is useful or a problem.

♦ ♦ ♦

CYCLE TIME:

Politics is a numbers game. The goal is to position yourself to win votes as quickly and easily as possible.

Related Articles from *Sun Tzu's Playbook*

In his second chapter, Sun Tzu teaches basic competitive economics. We explore these ideas in more detail in our **Sun Tzu's Warrior's Playbook** *To learn the step-by-step techniques for economical political campaigning, we recommend the articles listed below.*

1.3.1 Competitive Comparison: competition as the comparison of positions.

1.6.1 Shared Mission: finding goals that others can share.

1.8.3 Cycle Time: speed in feedback and reaction.

1.8.4 Probabilistic Process: the role of chance in strategic processes and systems.

2.2.1 Personal Relationships: how information depends on personal relationships.

2.2.2 Mental Models: how mental models simplify decision-making.

2.3.4 Using Questions: using questions in gathering information and predicting reactions.

3.1 Strategic Economics: balancing the cost and benefits of positioning.

3.1.1 Resource Limitations: the inherent limitation of strategic resources.

3.1.2 Strategic Profitability: understanding gains and losses.

3.1.3 Conflict Cost: the costly nature of resolving competitive comparisons by conflict.

Chapter 3

Planning an Attack: Your Political Ground

This chapter offers invaluable lessons on focusing your efforts. The central topic of this chapter is unity and focus and their effect on strength and power.

For Sun Tzu, unity and strength are not two separate ideas but a single idea, the concept of oneness. Oneness means both uniting with others and having a clear single purpose. This chapter's first lesson is that you must use the power of oneness at every level to successfully create a campaign.

A campaign must advance your political position. Advancing a position is what Sun Tzu meant by an attack. Strategic agility is the skill of advancing positions. In the second section, Sun Tzu lists the forms of advancing a position in descending order of effectiveness.

Sun Tzu teaches an incremental approach to advancing your political position. You focus on small, simple comparisons with the opponents where you have the clear advantage.

Are you a politician or a political idealist? In its fourth section, the chapter warns against idealistic thinking and explains how that thinking weakens your competitive strength.

Sun Tzu then details the five areas of knowledge that you must focus on to be successful, summarizing the main issues in the book thus far.

The chapter ends by explaining how successful strategy depends on understanding your relative position in the voter's mind.

Planning an Attack

UNITY:

*Strategy teaches
that the size of
an organization
is not nearly as
important as
how united it is.*

SUN TZU SAID:

Everyone relies on the arts of war. 1
A united nation is strong.
A divided nation is weak.
A united army is strong.
A divided army is weak.
A united force is strong.
A divided force is weak.
United men are strong.
Divided men are weak.
A united unit is strong.
A divided unit is weak.

[12]Unity works because it enables you to win
every battle you fight.
Still, this is the foolish goal of a weak leader.
Avoid battle and make the enemy's men surrender.
This is the right goal for a superior leader.

The best way to make war is to upset the enemy's plans. 2
The next best is to disrupt alliances.
The next best is to attack the opposing army.
The worst is to attack the enemy's cities.

Your Political Ground

THE CAMPAIGNER HEARS:

1 Every election depends on positioning.
A united political party is strong.
A divided political party is vulnerable.
A focused campaign is strong.
An unfocused campaign is vulnerable.
A popular political position is strong.
A minority political position is vulnerable.
A united supporter base is strong.
A divided supporter base is vulnerable.
A unified message works well.
A mixed message works poorly.

FOCUS:

*A political cam-
paign depends
upon a clear,
focused
message.*

Unity works because it enables you to win in
every election battle.
Still, winning election battles should never be your goal.
Pick vulnerable opponents and make their supporters give up.
This is the highest goal of the campaigner.

2 It's best to outmaneuver others for an open seat.
The next best approach is to win the support of key voter groups.
The next best is to run a better campaign on the issues.
The worst is to criticize an incumbent's past supporters.

This is what happens when you attack a city.

You can attempt it, but you can't finish it.

First you must make siege engines.

ATTACKS:

In classical strategy, an attack is any form of invading an opponent's territory. It is not fighting with competitors.

You need the right equipment and machinery.

It takes three months and still you cannot win.

Then you try to encircle the area.

You use three more months without making progress.

Your command still doesn't succeed and this angers you.

You then try to swarm the city.

This kills a third of your officers and men.

You are still unable to draw the enemy out of the city.

This attack is a disaster.

Make good use of war. **3**

Make the enemy's troops surrender.

You can do this fighting only minor battles.

You can draw their men out of their cities.

You can do it with small attacks.

You can destroy the men of a nation.

You must keep your campaign short.

DECISION:

Good strategic decisions are based on seeing how these five factors together create your position.

8You must be united in conflict from the top to the bottom.

Never stop when you are at war.

Your opportunity comes from being united.

In every situation, this is how your plan your attack as well.

What happens when you attack an electorate's past voting?

You create resistance that works against you.

First, you must point out mistakes in the past.

You need to use the right arguments and insights. This requires costly advertising and still you won't win their votes.

You then try to discredit past political decisions. You will waste more time and still not convince them.

When you fall behind in the polls, you will become frustrated.

You then try to outspend your opponent.

This destroys the financial base of your campaign.

The result is that you fail to win over the voters you wanted.

This type of campaigning is a disaster.

DISASTER:

Trying to convince voters that they made the wrong decision is a costly disaster just waiting to happen.

3 Make good use of politics.

Discourage your opponents' supporters.

You can do this by embarrassing them a little.

You can lure voters away from past political views.

You can leverage small changes in the political climate.

Undermine opponents' support from their party.

You must keep your campaign simple.

You must be totally devoted to a campaign, using all your resources.

Never stop working when in an election.

You can gain a dominant political position.

To do this, you must select the best campaign tactics.

UNITY:

Voters cannot remember all the details, but they will remember if you offer a complete picture.

¹²The rules for making war are:

If you outnumber enemy forces ten to one, surround them.

If you outnumber them five to one, attack them.

If you outnumber them two to one, divide them.

If you are equal, then find an advantageous battle.

If you are fewer, defend against them.

If you are much weaker, evade them.

¹⁹Small forces are not powerful.

However, large forces cannot catch them.

You must master command. 4

The nation must support you.

³Supporting the military makes the nation powerful.

Not supporting the military makes the nation weak.

⁵The army's position is made more difficult by politicians in three different ways.

Ignorant of the whole army's inability to advance, they order an advance.

Ignorant of the whole army's inability to withdraw, they order a withdrawal.

We call this tying up the army.

Politicians don't understand the army's business.

Still, they think they can run an army.

This confuses the army's officers.

The rules for campaign tactics are:

If you are an incumbent and trends favor you, just ask for votes.
If you are a challenger and trends favor you, attack opponents.
If you are an incumbent with a slight edge, split opposing forces.
If you are a challenger with a slight edge, focus on your issues.
If you are an incumbent and behind, hold existing supporters.
If you are a challenger and behind, keep raising new issues.

Challengers lack the power of incumbency.
But incumbents cannot take new positions like challengers can.

4 You must be decisive.
Your political party must support you.

Supporting the best candidates makes a political party powerful.
Failing to support the best candidates makes a political party weak.

The campaign's position is made difficult by political idealists in three ways.
Ignorant of a campaign's inability to win some voters, idealists want you to convert them.
Ignorant of how you need to win other voters, they want you to turn your back on them.
We call this hamstringing your campaign.
Idealists don't understand the tactics of a campaign.
Still, they think they can direct a campaign.
This confuses your political supporters.

¹²Politicians don't know the army's chain of command.
They give the army too much freedom.
This will create distrust among the army's officers.

¹⁵The entire army becomes confused and distrusting.
This invites invasion by many different rivals.
We say correctly that disorder in an army kills victory.

You must know five things to win: **5**
Victory comes from knowing when to attack and when to avoid battle.
Victory comes from correctly using both large and small forces.
Victory comes from everyone sharing the same goals.
Victory comes from finding opportunities in problems.
Victory comes from having a capable commander and the government leaving him alone.
You must know these five things.
You then know the theory of victory.

We say: **6**
"Know yourself and know your enemy.
You will be safe in every battle.
You may know yourself but not know the enemy.
You will then lose one battle for every one you win.
You may not know yourself or the enemy.
You will then lose every battle."

Idealists don't understand a campaign's priorities.
They want the campaign to accomplish too much.
This will create unrest among your campaign's workers.

An unfocused campaign becomes confused and uncertain.
This invites criticism from all political segments.
We say that a lack of focus in the campaign kills elections.

5 You must know five things to win elections:
Campaign success comes from knowing which races to enter and which to avoid.
Campaign success comes from correctly using both big issues and little ones.
Campaign success comes from sharing the majority's values.
Campaign success comes from seeing the opportunities in change.
Campaign success comes from having a capable candidate and avoiding ideological purity.
Master these five categories of knowledge.
You then know the secrets of winning elections.

6 A campaigner hears:
Know your position and your opponent's position with voters.
You will be safe in every election.
You may know your position but not your opponent's.
Then, for every vote you win, you will lose another.
You may know neither your position nor your opponent's.
Then you will lose every election.

◆ ◆ ◆

Related Articles from *Sun Tzu's Playbook*

In this third chapter, Sun Tzu introduces the basics of advancing into new areas. To learn the step-by-step techniques involved, we recommend the Sun Tzu's Warrior's Playbook *articles listed below.*

1.1.1 Position Dynamics: how all current positions are always getting better or worse.

1.1.2 Defending Positions: how we defend our current positions until new positions are established.

1.2 Subobjective Positions: the subjective and objective aspects of a position.

1.3.1 Competitive Comparison: competition as the comparison of positions.

1.7 Competitive Power: the sources of superiority in challenges.

1.7.1 Team Unity: strength by joining with others.

1.7.2 Goal Focus: strength as arising from concentrating efforts.

1.8 Progress Cycle: the adaptive loop by which positions are advanced.

1.8.1 Creation and Destruction: the creation and destruction of competitive positions.

1.8.2 The Adaptive Loop: the continual reiteration of position analysis.

2.3.6 Promises and Threats: the use of promises and threats as strategic moves.

2.4 Contact Networks: the range of contacts needed to create perspective.

2.4.1 Ground Perspective: getting information on a new competitive arena.

2.4.2 Climate Perspective: getting perspective on temporary external conditions.

3.0.0 Identifying Opportunities: the use of opportunities to advance a position.

3.1.3 Conflict Cost: the costly nature of resolving competitive comparisons by conflict.

3.2 Opportunity Creation: how change creates opportunities.

3.2.2 Opportunity Invisibility: why opportunities are always hidden.

3.2.4 Emptiness and Fullness: the transformations between strength and weakness.

3.4 Dis-Economies of Scale: how opportunities are created by the size of others.

3.4.2 Opportunity Fit: finding new opportunities that fit your size.

3.4.3 Reaction Lag: how size creates temporary openings.

3.5 Strength and Weakness: openings created by the strength of others.

3.6 Leveraging Subjectivity: openings between subjective and objective positions.

3.7 Defining the Ground: redefining a competitive arena to create relative mismatches.

5.6 Defensive Advances: balancing defending and advancing positions.

Chapter 4

Positioning: Positions on Issues

Sun Tzu's strategy requires finding ways to advance your position with voters rather than fighting political opponents. His concept of positioning arises from comparisons. Supporters and voters compare your offering with their alternative choices of candidates.

Sun Tzu starts the chapter by explaining that we can move to a new position only when an opportunity presents itself. You do not create a good opportunity to get elected. It must arise naturally.

In the second section, the text explains that before you can run for election, you have work to do. You must start positioning yourself so that you can be credible in a campaign. You must be able to defend yourself as the best candidate (or campaigner). This means you must first get to know and get known by the political influencers in an area.

The third section explains that after you see an opportunity to run, you must find a way to run easily and effortlessly. This requires the ability to adjust your political positions to the weaknesses of your potential opponents.

In the fourth section, Sun Tzu provides a simple formula for calculating what issues and positions you must take to win a given election. This is based upon the demographics of the region in which you are running.

In the final section, Sun Tzu briefly explains how good positioning leads to winning the key supporters or influencers that win elections. You use these influencers to win the voters.

Positioning

SUN TZU SAID:

Learn from the history of successful battles. 1
First, you should control the situation not try to win.
If you adjust to the enemy, you will find a way to win.
The opportunity to win does not come from you.
The opportunity to win comes from your enemy.

[6]You must pick good battles.
You can control them until you can win.
You cannot win them until the enemy enables
your victory.

[9]We say:
You see the opportunity for victory; you don't
control it.

DEFENSE:

Strategy teaches that you must first make sure that your existing position is secure before moving to a new one.

Positions on Issues

THE CAMPAIGNER HEARS:

1 Learn from what works in successful elections.
Your first actions should pick the right races, not beat an opponent.
As you adjust to opponents, you will find a way to win the election.
The opportunity to win doesn't come from your position.
The opportunity comes from the weaknesses of your opponent.

You must pick the right elections.
You can stay competitive in them until you can win.
You cannot win an election if your opponent leaves you no opening.

Pay attention:
You must find the elections you can win; you can't create them.

OPENINGS:

Campaigns must take advantage of opportunities in the process that your opponents create for you.

You are sometimes unable to win. 2
You must then defend.
You will eventually be able to win.
You must then attack.
Defend when you have insufficient strength.
Attack when you have a surplus of strength.

7You must defend yourself well.
Save your forces and dig in.
You must attack well.
Move your forces when you have a clear advantage.

11You must always protect yourself until you can completely triumph.

Some may see how to win. 3
However, they cannot move their forces where they must.
This demonstrates limited ability.

4Some can struggle to a victory and the whole world may praise their winning.
This also demonstrates a limited ability.

6Win as easily as picking up a fallen hair.
Don't use all of your forces.
See the time to move.
Don't try to find something clever.
Hear the clap of thunder.
Don't try to hear something subtle.

2 The ground and climate can be against you.
Build up your position to get in a position to run.
Eventually, the ground and climate will be in your favor.
You must then advance to an active campaign.
Build your position when the election odds are not in your favor.
Advance to a campaign when all the factors are in your favor.

You must build up your political position carefully.
Save your resources and become known in the community.
You must advance your positions well.
Move to positions that have a clear advantage in the election.

You must always maintain your electability until you find an election in which you can dominate.

3 Some may see an election they can win.
Yet they cannot establish their position to run in that election.
This shows a limited ability.

Some politicians can win tough elections, and everyone will praise them.
This also shows a limited ability.

The best elections are effortless.
Avoid using all your resources.
Vision is seeing what is obvious.
Don't try to fabricate positions.
Hearing the voter is easy if you listen.
Don't imagine what you want to hear.

¹²Learn from the history of successful battles.
Victory goes to those who make winning easy.
A good battle is one that you will obviously win.
It doesn't take intelligence to win a reputation.
It doesn't take courage to achieve success.

¹⁷You must win your battles without effort.
Avoid difficult struggles.
Fight when your position must win.
You always win by preventing your defeat.

²¹You must engage only in winning battles.
Position yourself where you cannot lose.
Never waste an opportunity to defeat your enemy.

²⁴You win a war by first assuring yourself of victory.
Only afterward do you look for a fight.
Outmaneuver the enemy before the first battle and then
fight to win.

BATTLE:

In Sun Tzu's terms, battle means the point at which opponents are compared not simply conflict.

Learn from successful campaigns.
Winning votes requires making the choice easy.
A good campaign is one that you will obviously win.
You don't have to be a genius to win a good reputation.
You don't have to be courageous to win elections.

You want to win elections without problems.
Avoid difficult races.
Run for election when your positions must win.
You always win by maintaining your credibility.

You must engage only in winnable elections.
Position yourself where the majority of voters will vote for you.
Never waste an chance to win open seats from weak opponents.

You win office by first assuring yourself of electability.
Only then do you look for a political race.
Outmaneuver your opponents before the primary and then campaign to win.

IDENTITY:

Voters need to know who you are, but only in terms of what you can do to meet their needs.

You must make good use of war. **4**
Study military philosophy and the art of defense.
You can control your victory or defeat.

[4]This is the art of war:
"1.   Discuss the distances.
2.   Discuss your numbers.
3.   Discuss your calculations.
4.   Discuss your decisions.
5.   Discuss victory.

[10]The ground determines the distance.
The distance determines your numbers.
Your numbers determine your calculations.
Your calculations determine your decisions.
Your decisions determine your victory."

[15]Creating a winning war is like balancing a coin of gold
against a coin of silver.
Creating a losing war is like balancing a coin of silver
against a coin of gold.

Winning a battle is always a matter of people. **5**
You pour them into battle like a flood of water pouring into
a deep gorge.
This is a matter of positioning.

♦ ♦ ♦

4 You must make good use of election information.
Study election outcomes and what type of candidates win.
You can control campaign success or failure.

The art of politics requires:
1. Discussing voter demographics.
2. Discussing numbers of supporters.
3. Discussing turnout calculations.
4. Discussion the positioning decision.
5. Discussing political success.

The electoral area determines voter demographics.
The demographics determine numbers of potential supporters.
The number of supporters determines your turnout calculations.
These calculations determines decisions about political positions.
Your political decisions determine your victory.

Creating a winning campaign is a matter of pitting a strong position against weak ones.
Creating a losing campaign is a matter of taking a weak position in the face of stronger ones.

5 Winning a campaign is always a matter of supporters.
You pour your supporters into an election to influence other people like themselves to vote for you.
This is a matter of your political positioning.

♦ ♦ ♦

Related Articles from *Sun Tzu's Playbook*

In this fourth chapter, Sun Tzu explains the process for advancing positions. To learn the step-by-step techniques involved, we recommend the Sun Tzu's Warrior's Playbook *articles listed below.*

1.1.2 Defending Positions: how we defend our current positions until new positions are established.

1.2 Subobjective Positions: the subjective and objective aspects of a position.

1.3.1 Competitive Comparison: competition as the comparison of positions.

1.7 Competitive Power: the sources of superiority in challenges.

1.8 Progress Cycle: the adaptive loop by which positions are advanced.

1.8.1 Creation and Destruction: the creation and destruction of competitive positions.

1.8.2 The Adaptive Loop: the continual reiteration of position analysis.

3.0.0 Identifying Opportunities: the use of opportunities to advance a position.

3.2 Opportunity Creation: how change creates opportunities.

3.2.4 Emptiness and Fullness: the transformations between strength and weakness.

3.4.2 Opportunity Fit: finding new opportunities that fit your size.

3.5 Strength and Weakness: openings created by the strength of others.

3.7 Defining the Ground: redefining a competitive arena to create relative mismatches.

5.6 Defensive Advances: balancing defending and advancing positions.

5.6.1 Defense Priority: why defense has first claim on our resources.

9.4 Crisis Defense: how vulnerabilities are exploited and defended during a crisis.

9.4.1 Division Defense: preventing organizational division during a crisis.

9.4.2 Panic Defense: the mistakes arising from panic during a crisis.

9.4.3 Defending Openings: how to defend openings created by a crisis.

9.4.4 Defending Alliances: dealing with guilt by association.

9.4.5 Defensive Balance: using short-term conditions to tip the balance in a crisis.

Chapter 5

Momentum: Creative Campaigning

In the world of politics, Sun Tzu's concept of momentum provides a powerful tool for winning campaigns. To create momentum as a force for change, you must alternate between well-understood positions with which the voter is comfortable and political positions that are novel and surprising. A creative campaign, one that injects novel ideas into a standard campaign, creates political momentum.

In the chapter's first section, Sun Tzu explains that every type of campaign is basically the same. You try to leverage strengths against weaknesses in a surprising way.

The second section explains that predictability and surprise depend on one another. To impress voters with new viewpoints, you must first prepare them using ideas with which they are comfortable. You then use surprise to take control of the campaign's direction.

Sun Tzu uses the third section of this chapter to explain that momentum creates emotion to motivate people. We use the right timing to release the tension created by surprise.

The fourth section says that elections are inherently confusing, but you can take control of the flow of issues by using planned surprises to which others must adapt.

In the final section, the issue is communicating the surprise through your people on the street, your supporters. You must use them to share their excitement to win broad support.

Momentum

You control a large group the same as you control a few. 1
You just divide their ranks correctly.
You fight a large army the same as you fight a small one.
You only need the right position and communication.
You may meet a large enemy army.
You must be able to sustain an enemy attack without being defeated.
You must correctly use both surprise and direct action.
Your army's position must increase your strength.

Troops flanking an enemy can smash them like eggs.
You must correctly use both strength and weakness.

It is the same in all battles. 2
You use a direct approach to engage the enemy.
You use surprise to win.

STANDARDS:

To develop momentum you first need a set of standards that others can depend upon.

⁴You must use surprise for a successful escape.
Surprise is as infinite as the weather and land.
Surprise is as inexhaustible as the flow of a river.

78 *The Art of War 5: Momentum*

Creative Campaigning

THE CAMPAIGNER HEARS:

1 Complex campaigns are the same as simple ones.
You only need to divide your time among more people.
Campaigns against incumbents are like those against challengers.
You only need the right issues and a way to communicate them.
You may meet better-financed opponents.
You must always be able to withstand their attacks without faltering.
You must use both surprising and expected campaign moves.
Your campaign position must emphasize your appeal.
You can blindside opponents and destroy their credibility.
You must pit your political strength against their weaknesses.

2 It is the same in every campaign.
You campaign predictably to create an opponent's expectations.
You then do something surprising to win.

You can use surprise to recover from missteps.
Use the unique conditions in every campaign.
Changes in the political climate are endless.

CREATIVITY:

All elections are the same and all are unique. Open with what is expected and finish with the unexpected.

7You can be stopped and yet recover the initiative.
You must use your days and months correctly.

9If you are defeated, you can recover.
You must use the four seasons correctly.

11There are only a few notes in the scale.
Yet you can always rearrange them.
You can never hear every song of victory.

14There are only a few basic colors.
Yet you can always mix them.
You can never see all the shades of victory.

17There are only a few flavors.
Yet you can always blend them.
You can never taste all the flavors of victory.

20You fight with momentum.
There are only a few types of surprises and direct actions.
Yet you can always vary the ones you use.
There is no limit to the ways you can win.

24Surprise and direct action give birth to each other.
They are like a circle without end.
You cannot exhaust all their possible combinations!

Surging water flows together rapidly. 3
Its pressure washes away boulders.
This is momentum.

You can encounter obstacles and yet regain the upper hand.
You must use your campaign timetable effectively.

You can lose polls and still win elections.
You must adjust to the cyclical nature of campaigns.

There are only a few basic voter concerns.
Yet you can combine them in any number of ways.
You will never exhaust the issues that win elections.

There are only a few basic types of political opportunities.
Yet every political contest offers a unique combination.
You will never find all the ways to win in an election.

There are only a few kinds of political appeals.
Yet you can always mix them in new ways.
You can never discover all the winning positions.

You campaign by controlling the force of change.
You need only a few creative twists with your standard techniques.
Yet you combine them to make each campaign unique.
You have no limit to the ways you can win an election.

Doing what everyone expects creates the potential for a surprise.
Each unexpected move is the new foundation for campaigning.
You cannot run out of exciting moves to make!

3 Getting emotions flowing gives impact to ideas.
The force of people's emotions can wash away resistance.
This creates campaign momentum.

4A hawk suddenly strikes a bird.
Its contact alone kills the prey.
This is timing.

7You must fight only winning battles.
Your momentum must be overwhelming.
Your timing must be exact.

10Your momentum is like the tension of a bent crossbow.
Your timing is like the pulling of a trigger.

War is very complicated and confusing. 4
Battle is chaotic.
Nevertheless, you must not allow chaos.

4War is very sloppy and messy.
Positions turn around.
Nevertheless, you must never be defeated.

7Chaos gives birth to control.
Fear gives birth to courage.
Weakness gives birth to strength.

MOMENTUM:

*Dependable
standards
and constant
improvement
create pressure
to decide in your
favor.*

10You must control chaos.
This depends on your planning.
Your men must brave their fears.
This depends on their momentum.

14You have strengths and weaknesses.
These come from your position.

A twist at the right time penetrates the voters' mind.
Its shock alone can change their opinions.
This is timing.

You must invest only in winning campaigns.
Your shifts in emphasis must be impossible to ignore.
You must time your surprises exactly.

A change in focus increases the pressure in the campaign.
You time your surprises to unleash that pressure.

4 Elections are always complicated and confusing.
Campaigning is messy.
It is your job to control its focus.

Campaign positions are never neat and tidy.
They are constantly shifting.
Nevertheless, you must never be outmaneuvered.

The voters' confusion gives you power.
Their timidity allows your audacity.
Your opponents' weaknesses are your strength.

CONTROL:

You must clarify what is confusing.
This depends on your simple message.
Your supporters must overcome their fears.
This depends on your campaign momentum.

*You cannot con-
trol voters, but
you can prepare
for the predict-
able pitfalls in
the campaign
process.*

You appeal to some voters but not to others.
Your appeal arises from your political position.

¹⁶You must force the enemy to move to your advantage.

Use your position.

The enemy must follow you.

Surrender a position.

The enemy must take it.

You can offer an advantage to move him.

You can use your men to move him.

You can use your strength to hold him.

You want a successful battle. 5

To do this, you must seek momentum.

Do not just demand a good fight from your people.

You must pick good people and then give them momentum.

⁵You must create momentum.

You create it with your men during battle.

This is comparable to rolling trees and stones.

Trees and stones roll because of their shape and weight.

Offer men safety and they will stay calm.

Endanger them and they will act.

Give them a place and they will hold.

Round them up and they will march.

¹³You make your men powerful in battle with momentum.

This should be like rolling round stones down over a high, steep cliff.

Momentum is critical.

✦ ✦ ✦

You must force opponents into positions that broaden your appeal.
Leverage your political position.
Opponents must adjust to it.
Give up opposing them on a minor issue.
Your opponents must applaud you.
Bait your opponents into shifting on major issues.
Use your support to lure them into flip-flopping.
You must use your simple message to counter them.

5 You desire a winning campaign.
To win, you must find ways to create campaign momentum.
Do not just demand a good effort from your supporters.
You must win good people and arm them with the force of change.

You must create a flow of issues.
You do this to win supporters during the campaign.
You must know what motivates different types of people.
People are motivated by their conditions and needs.
Make supporters comfortable to keep them happy.
Make them fearful and they will take action.
Give them a positive image and they will stay.
Organize them and they will work for you.

You make supporters powerful in politics with the force of change.
You want everything moving inevitably toward a decision in your favor.
Controlling campaign issues is critical.

Related Articles from *Sun Tzu's Playbook*

In his fifth chapter, Sun Tzu explains the process for creating momentum. To learn the step-by-step techniques involved, we recommend the Sun Tzu's Warrior's Playbook articles listed below.

1.2 Subobjective Positions: the subjective and objective aspects of a position.

7.0 Creating Momentum: how momentum requires creativity.

7.1 Order from Chaos: the value of chaos in creating competitive momentum.

7.1.1 Creating Surprise: creating surprise using our chaotic environment.

7.1.2 Momentum Psychology: the psychology of surprise.

7.1.3 Standards and Innovation: the methodology of creativity.

7.2 Standards First: the role of standards in creating connections with others.

7.2.1 Proven Methods: identifying and recognizing the limits of best practices.

7.2.2 Preparing Expectations: how we shape other people's expectations.

7.3 Strategic Innovation: a simple system for innovation.

7.3.1 Expected Elements: dividing processes and systems into components.

7.3.2 Elemental Rearrangement: seeing invention as rearranging proven elements.

7.3.3 Creative Innovation: the more advanced methods for innovation.

7.4 Competitive Timing: the role of timing in creating momentum.

7.4.1 Timing Methods: the three simplest methods of controlling timing.

7.4.2 Momentum Timing: the relative value of momentum at various times in a campaign.

7.4.3 Interrupting Patterns: how repetition creates patterns for surprise.

7.5 Momentum Limitations: the implications of momentum's temporary nature.

7.5.1 Momentum Conversion: converting momentum into positions with more value.

7.5.2 The Spread of Innovation: the spread of innovation to advance our position.

7.6 Productive Competition: using momentum to produce more resources.

7.6.1 Resource Discovery: using innovation to create value from seemingly worthless resources.

7.6.2 Ground Creation: the creation of new competitive ground to be successful.

Chapter 6

Weakness and Strength: Your Voters' Needs

Weaknesses are both 1) issues the different voter groups within the electorate care about and 2) issues your political opponents overlook. Your strength comes from these weaknesses.

In the first section, Sun Tzu begins to clarify this complex idea by explaining that if you are the first to raise a key issue to a particular voter group, you are naturally stronger than if you get to a group of voters after competitors do.

The second section continues this idea by explaining that you can make progress more quickly by addressing issues that are overlooked by your political opponents.

In the third section, Sun Tzu explains the need to keep your campaign activities and positions on issues secret.

The fourth section teaches you to focus on your weakest opponents in a primary first to win their supporters.

In the fifth section, the topic is how we avoid being pigeonholed by the opposition by keeping our true political orientation a secret. The goal is to win voters using our positions on issues while confusing opponents based on these same issues.

Sun Tzu discusses electoral mathematics in the sixth section of this chapter. A winning candidate stitches together a winning coalition out of a number of smaller, less visible voter groups.

In the final two sections, the text explains how you must understand each voter group on which you focus. However, you must only take positions on issues that allow you to remain flexible.

Weakness and Strength

SUN TZU SAID:

Always arrive first to the empty battlefield to await the 1
enemy at your leisure.
After the battleground is occupied and you hurry to it,
fighting is more difficult.

3You want a successful battle.
Move your men, but not into opposing forces.

5You can make the enemy come to you.
Offer him an advantage.
You can make the enemy avoid coming to you.
Threaten him with danger.

9When the enemy is fresh, you can tire him.
When he is well fed, you can starve him.
When he is relaxed, you can move him.

WEAKNESS:

*Competitors'
weaknesses
arise naturally
from unsatisfied
needs. Needs
create opportu-
nities.*

Your Voters' Needs

THE CAMPAIGNER HEARS:

1 Identify unmet voter needs as issues before your political opposition does.
After opponents stake out their positions on an issue, contesting that issue is harder.

You want a successful contest on voter needs.
Have your supporters work, but not on the same old issues.

You can make opponents support your issue.
Make it clear that it strengthens their position.
You can keep opponents from supporting your issue.
Make it clear that it weakens their position.

If an issue refreshes an opponent, wear it out.
If an issue wins donations, take it away.
If your opponents like their position, move them.

STRENGTHS:

Your strengths make it easier for you to make some appeals that your opponents cannot match.

Leave any place without haste. 2
Hurry to where you are unexpected.
You can easily march hundreds of miles without tiring.
To do so, travel through areas that are deserted.
You must take whatever you attack.
Attack when there is no defense.
You must have walls to defend.
Defend where it is impossible to attack.

AVOIDANCE:

*Success depends
upon avoiding
competitive
challenges while
you move to
develop better
positions.*

9Be skilled in attacking.
Give the enemy no idea where to defend.

11Be skillful in your defense.
Give the enemy no idea where to attack.

Be subtle! Be subtle! 3
Arrive without any clear formation.
Ghostly! Ghostly!
Arrive without a sound.
You must use all your skill to control the enemy's decisions.

6Advance quietly and he can't defend.
Charge through his openings.
Withdraw quietly and he cannot chase you.
Move quickly so that he cannot catch you.

2 Abandon any political position gradually.
Be quick to raise new, unexpected issues.
You can move through many unexplored issues quickly and easily.
You must use issues that others have overlooked.
You must win votes with every issue you advance.
Advance issues that change voters' minds.
You must hold voters when you've won them.
Choose positions that opponents cannot counter.

You must be skilled in advancing new issues.
Give opponents no clue about where to defend.

You must be skilled in holding supporters.
Leave no obvious places to challenge your issues.

SPECIALIZE:

Focus your efforts on winning issues that are difficult for opponents to duplicate.

3 You must be elusive.
Start without any clear agenda.
You can be enigmatic.
Listen before you talk.
You must use all your skill to control your opponents' choices.

Work behind the scenes with forgotten voter groups.
Work hard where others are not working.
Withdraw quietly so your opposition cannot copy you.
Move quickly so opponents cannot catch up.

[10]Always pick your own battles.
The enemy can hide behind high walls and deep trenches.
Do not try to win by fighting him directly.
Instead, attack a place that he must recapture.
Avoid the battles that you don't want.
You can divide the ground and yet defend it.
Don't give the enemy anything to win.
Divert him by coming to where you defend.

Make other men take a position while you take none. 4
Then focus your forces where the enemy divides his forces.
Where you focus, you unite your forces.
When the enemy divides, he creates many small groups.
You want your large group to attack one of his small ones.
Then you have many men where the enemy has but a few.
Your larger force can overwhelm his smaller one.
Then go on to the next small enemy group.
You can take them one at a time.

You must keep the place that you have chosen as a 5
battleground a secret.
The enemy must not know.
Force the enemy to prepare his defense in
many places.

SECRECY:

You cannot exploit the weakness of your opponents if everyone knows what you are doing.

You want the enemy to defend many places.
Then you can choose where to fight.
His forces will be weak there.

You must pick the right issues to emphasize.

Your opponents can hide behind their positions on safe issues.

You need not go after them directly.

Instead, take positions on issues on which they must also take a stand.

Avoid the comparisons that you don't want.

You can divide the voters and still defend your positions.

Don't give political opponents any potential supporters to win.

They must leave their safe positions to counter you.

4 In a primary, let your opponents take positions before you do.

Then focus your efforts on where your opponents divide the voters.

Focus where you can unite your supporters.

Where opponents divide supporters they create small groups.

You want a plurality where opponents have a minority.

You want many supporters in areas where opponents have few.

Your many supporters can then convert your weakest opponent's group.

Then move on to the next weakest opponents.

You can take on opponents one at a time.

5 Before a general election, you must keep your campaign focus a secret.

Your opponent must misjudge you.

Encourage opponents to defend on every possible issue.

You want them to spread themselves too thin.

You can then choose the key focus you desire.

You focus where they are weakest.

ADAPTABILITY:

Campaigning is not the execution of a plan but constantly adjusting to openings in voter needs.

7If he reinforces his front lines, he depletes his rear.
If he reinforces his rear, he depletes his front.
If he reinforces his right flank, he depletes his left.
If he reinforces his left flank, he depletes his
right.

WEAK POINTS:

*You must see
a competitor's
most serious
weak points
and focus your
strengths on
exploiting them.*

Without knowing the place of attack, he
cannot prepare.
Without knowing the right place, he will be
weak everywhere.

13The enemy has weak points.
Prepare your men against them.
He has strong points.
Make his men prepare themselves against you.

You must know the battleground. 6
You must know the time of battle.
You can then travel a thousand miles and still win the battle.

4The enemy should not know the battleground.
He shouldn't know the time of battle.
His left flank will be unable to support his right.
His right will be unable to support his left.
His front lines will be unable to support his rear.
His rear will be unable to support his front.
His support is distant even if it is only ten miles away.
What unknown place can be close?

If opponents want more government, they sacrifice personal liberty.
If they focus on personal liberty, they are weakening society.
If they focus on traditional values, they are weak on new ideas.
If they focus on new ideas, they are weak on traditional values.
Without knowing your focus, they cannot fight you directly.
If they claim every position, they are weak everywhere.

All voters have unmet needs.
Prepare positions on issues to address those needs.
Opponents can satisfy some voters.
Encourage them to be all things to all people.

NEEDS:

Voters have an infinite number of needs. You must choose those that you can best address.

6 Know where the majority of votes are.
You must organize your campaign timetable.
You can then convince many voter groups and win the election.

Your opponents must not know which voters you are after.
They must never know your campaign timetable.
They should be too far left for your voter groups on the right.
They should be too far right for your voter groups on the left.
Their campaign workers should be at odds with your voter groups.
Your voters groups should be at odds with their volunteers.
Their supporters should keep their distance even if politically close.
If they do not know your campaign focus, how can they fight you?

¹²You control the balance of forces.
The enemy may have many men but they are superfluous.
How can they help him to victory?

¹⁵We say:
You must let victory happen.

¹⁷The enemy may have many men.
You can still control him without a fight.

When you form your strategy, know the strengths and 7
weaknesses of your plan.
When you execute a plan, know how to manage both action
and inaction.
When you take a position, know the deadly and the winning
grounds.
When you enter into battle, know when you have too many
or too few men.

⁵Use your position as your war's centerpiece.
Arrive at the battle without a formation.
Don't take a position in advance.
Then even the best spies can't report it.
Even the wisest general cannot plan to counter you.
Take a position where you can triumph using superior numbers.
Keep opposing forces ignorant.
Everyone should learn your location after your position has
given you success.
No one should know how your location gives you a winning
position.

You decide the balance of power when you pick voters to court.
Opponents can have many supporters and still have a minority.
How can they get your opponent elected?

Sun Tzu teaches:
You must let a majority arise.

Political opponents may have many supporters.
You can still win a majority without fighting for them.

7 When you focus on a voter segment, know that group's desires and fears.
When you plan to contact them, know what needs to be done and what does not.
When you take a position on their issues, know its pitfalls and winning points.
When you campaign for them, know when you have enough or too few supporters to contact them.

Use your position on issues as your campaign's centerpiece.
Start your campaign without an ideological position.
Don't take positions too quickly.
Then people cannot categorize you.
Even the best campaigner cannot plan how to counter you.
Go after voter groups for which you can be the dominant champion.
Keep your opponents in the dark.
Competitors should only learn which voters you are after when you establish dominance.
Competitors should not know how you became so strong among any particular voter group.

Make a successful battle one from which the enemy cannot
recover.
You must continually adjust your position to his position.

Manage your military position like water. 8
Water takes every shape.
It avoids the high and moves to the low.
Your war can take any shape.
It must avoid the strong and strike the weak.
Water follows the shape of the land that directs its flow.
Your forces follow the enemy, who determines how you win.

8Make war without a standard approach.
Water has no consistent shape.
If you follow the enemy's shifts and changes, you can always
find a way to win.
We call this shadowing.

12Fight five different campaigns without a firm rule for victory.
Use all four seasons without a consistent position.
Your timing must be sudden.
A few weeks determine your failure or success.

✦ ✦ ✦

ADJUSTMENT:

*Continuously
adjust to con-
tinuous change.*

Make sure that opponents cannot steal the voter group back from you.

To protect your positions, adjust to your opponent's countermoves.

8 You must remain fluid in your political positioning.
Your campaign can take any shape.
Avoid the theoretical and move to what is practical.
Your issues can take any shape.
Avoid solid party voters and go after the undecided voters.
Communication channels shape your campaign and direct its flow.
Your campaign observes opponents and who they are not reaching.

You must avoid rigid campaign plans.
Good campaigns have no consistent shape.
You win elections by knowing your opponents' moves and adapting to the openings they leave.
This is called shadowing.

Use different campaign tactics; no single approach always wins.
Use a cycle of changing issues in your campaign.
You must always create a sense of urgency.
The weeks before the vote determine success or failure.

♦ ♦ ♦

URGENCY:

*Win the voters
you can quickly.*

Related Articles from *Sun Tzu's Playbook*

In chapter six, Sun Tzu explains how to find opportunities by leveraging opposites. To learn the step-by-step techniques involved, we recommend the Sun Tzu's Warrior's Playbook *articles listed below.*

1.2.1 Competitive Landscapes: the arenas in which rivals jockey for position.

1.2.2 Exploiting Exploration: how competitive landscapes are searched and positions utilized.

1.2.3 Position Complexity: how strategic positions arise from interactions in complex environments.

1.3.1 Competitive Comparison: competition as the comparison of positions.

2.4 Contact Networks: the range of contacts needed to create perspective.

2.4.1 Ground Perspective: getting information on a new competitive arena.

2.4.2 Climate Perspective: getting perspective on temporary external conditions.

2.4.3 Command Perspective: developing sources for understanding decision-makers.

2.4.4 Methods Perspective: developing contacts who understand best practices.

2.4.5 Mission Perspective: how we develop and use a perspective on motivation.

2.5 The Big Picture: building big-picture strategic awareness.

2.6 Knowledge Leverage: getting competitive value out of knowledge.

2.7 Information Secrecy: the role of limiting information in controlling relationships.

3.2.3 Complementary Opposites: the dynamics of balance from opposing forces.

3.2.4 Emptiness and Fullness: rules on the transformations between emptiness and fullness.

3.2.5 Dynamic Reversal: how situations reverse themselves naturally.

3.5 Strength and Weakness: six key methods regarding openings created by the strength of others.

3.6 Leveraging Subjectivity: openings between subjective and objective positions.

3.7 Defining the Ground: redefining a competitive arena to create relative mismatches.

3.8 Strategic Matrix Analysis: two-dimensional representations of strategic space.

4.7 Competitive Weakness: how certain opportunities can bring out our weaknesses.

4.7.1 Command Weaknesses: the character flaws of leaders and how to exploit them.

4.7.2 Group Weaknesses: organizational weakness and where groups fail.

6.7 Tailoring to Conditions: overcoming opposition using conditions in the environment.

6.7.1 Form Adjustments: adapting responses based on the form of the ground.

6.7.2 Size Adjustments: adapting responses based on comparing size of forces.

6.7.3 Strength Adjustments: adapting responses based on unity of opposing forces.

6.8 Competitive Psychology: improving competitive psychology even in adversity and failure.

6.8.1 Adversity and Creativity: how we use adversity to spark our creativity.

6.8.2 Strength in Adversity: using adversity to increase a group's unity and focus.

Chapter 7

Armed Conflict: Contacting Voters

All campaigns must focus on contacting voters. Voter contact is the source of not only voters but donations.

In this chapter's first section, Sun Tzu warns about acting as a typical politician. Sun Tzu's method, focusing on winning voters, requires a different, more creative form of contact.

In the second section, Sun Tzu discusses the hasty, sloppy ways that politicians contact voters. They make contact before they even know who they should be talking to and what they should be saying. This approach is counterproductive.

In the third section, Sun Tzu discusses the need to control perceptions. We apply these lessons to fund-raising, the type of voter contact that all other forms of voter contact depend upon.

In the next section, we discuss the fact that most campaigns are essentially boring. Boring people with your campaign positions is a poor investment of your donors' money.

In the fifth section, Sun Tzu discusses the importance of emotion in motivating an army. Since more voter contact takes place through volunteers, these lessons about how to manage emotions are critical.

In the chapter's final section, we address the common sense rules for communication. You have to pick the right time and place to contact voters. There are a number of mistakes that most people make winning supporters that you must learn how to avoid.

Armed Conflict

SUN TZU SAID:

Everyone uses the arts of war. 1
You accept orders from the government.
Then you assemble your army.
You organize your men and build camps.
You must avoid disasters from armed conflict.

[6]Seeking armed conflict can be disastrous.
Because of this, a detour can be the shortest path.
Because of this, problems can become
opportunities.

[9]Use an indirect route as your highway.
Use the search for advantage to guide you.
When you fall behind, you must catch up.
When you get ahead, you must wait.
You must know the detour that most directly
accomplishes your plan.

[14]Undertake armed conflict when you have an
advantage.
Seeking armed conflict for its own sake is
dangerous.

CONFLICT:

Strategy teaches that conflict is always costly so it must always be avoided whenever possible.

Contacting Voters

THE CAMPAIGNER HEARS:

1 Everyone uses the art of campaigning.
You decide to run at the behest of your supporters.
You then put together your campaign.
You organize your supporters and target certain voter groups.
You must then avoid mistakes in contacting the electorate.

Promoting yourself as a politician can be counterproductive.
Because of this, you look for different channels of communication.
You must find the opportunities hidden in every challenge.

You must find unique channels of communication.
Let your quest for certain types of voters guide you.
If you are less known, you must become known.
If you are well known, wait to contact them.

CONTACT:

You must find new avenues that get your message
to potential supporters.

*The difference
between good
campaigns and
great campaigns
is how well they
handle voter
contact.*

Only make contact with voters when you know
how to win them.
Promoting yourself without a message is worthless.

You can build up an army to fight for an advantage. 2
Then you won't catch the enemy.
You can force your army to go fight for an advantage.
Then you abandon your heavy supply wagons.

5You keep only your armor and hurry after the enemy.
You avoid stopping day or night.
You use many roads at the same time.
You go hundreds of miles to fight for an advantage.
Then the enemy catches your commanders and your army.
Your strong soldiers get there first.
Your weaker soldiers follow behind.
Using this approach, only one in ten will arrive.
You can try to go fifty miles to fight for an advantage.
Then your commanders and army will stumble.
Using this method, only half of your soldiers will make it.
You can try to go thirty miles to fight for an advantage.
Then only two out of three will get there.

18If you make your army travel without good
supply lines, your army will die.
Without supplies and food, your army will
die.
If you don't save the harvest, your army will
die.

FIGHTING:

You do not create opportunities by fighting for them. The use of force without strategy is wasted effort.

2 You can build a campaign to fight against political opponents. But you cannot make them less known.
You can force your supporters to go out and argue with voters.
But you then abandon your most important assets.

You can keep the political faith and rush into political combat.
You can work day and night.
You can contact voters in every medium available.
You can go everywhere to get your name known.
Then opponents will shape your positions with the voters.
Your name gets out to the voters first.
Your ability to deliver a meaningful message lags behind.
Only a small fraction of your efforts will result in votes.
You can try campaigning before targeting voter segments.
You will then stumble through your voter contacts.
You will only capture half your potential voters.
You can try to contact voters without volunteers.
You will only win two out of three potential votes.

If you campaign without a targeted message, your voter contact will fail.
Without communication and volunteers, voter contact will fail.
If you don't know your target voters, voter contact will fail.

GROUNDWORK:

Research your voters, opponents, and positions until your knowledge of the situation will win.

²¹Do not let any of your potential enemies know what you
are planning.
Still, you must not hesitate to form alliances.
You must know the mountains and forests.
You must know where the obstructions are.
You must know where the marshes are.
If you don't, you cannot move the army.
If you don't, you must use local guides.
If you don't, you can't take advantage of the terrain.

You make war by making a false stand. 3
By finding an advantage, you can move.
By dividing and joining, you can reinvent yourself and
transform the situation.
You can move as quickly as the wind.
You can rise like the forest.
You can invade and plunder like fire.
You can stay as motionless as a mountain.
You can be as mysterious as the fog.
You can strike like sounding thunder.

DECEPTION:

*Success comes
from control-
ling people's
perceptions by
shaping the way
situations must
appear to them.*

¹⁰Divide your troops to plunder the villages.
When on open ground, dividing is an
advantage.
Don't worry about organization; just move.
Be the first to find a new route that leads
directly to a winning plan.
This is how you are successful at armed
conflict.

Instead, you must not let your opponents know how you are campaigning.

You must not hesitate to find political alliances.

You must know the major voter groups and their issues.

You must know where the potential problem groups will be.

You must avoid getting bogged down.

If you do not, you cannot move your campaign.

If you do not, you need local supporters who can guide you.

If you do not, you cannot take advantage of the political situation.

3 You must raise money by pretending money is not an issue.

By finding a fund-raising edge, you can advance.

By dividing the donor base and adding new donors, you can get the money to transform an election.

You must contact donors more quickly than others can.

You must stand up and ask for money.

You can go outside an area and get the funds you can.

You can be patient in insisting on party support.

You can be silent on how much money you have.

You can make noise when the money is rolling in.

Divide up your volunteers to raise funds.

In overlooked donor areas, dividing is an advantage.

DIVISION:

Do not worry about organizing; just get out there.

You divide your efforts to find opportunities, and you must focus your efforts to exploit opportunities.

Be the first to discover a new source of funds that finances a winning campaign.

This is how you are successful at contacting voters.

Military experience says: 4
"You can speak, but you will not be heard.
You must use gongs and drums.
You cannot really see your forces just by looking.
You must use banners and flags."

6You must master gongs, drums, banners, and flags.
Place people as a single unit where they can all see and hear.
You must unite them as one.
Then the brave cannot advance alone.
The fearful cannot withdraw alone.
You must force them to act as a group.

12In night battles, you must use numerous fires and drums.
In day battles, you must use many banners and flags.
You must position your people to control what they see and hear.

You control your army by controlling its morale. 5
As a general, you must be able to control emotions.

3In the morning, a person's energy is high.
During the day, it fades.
By evening, a person's thoughts turn to home.
You must use your troops wisely.
Avoid the enemy's high spirits.
Strike when his men are lazy and want to go home.
This is how you master energy.

4 Experience in campaigning teaches us this:
"You can advertise, but you will not be heard.
You must be inventive to get people's attention.
You cannot be seen just by having a presence.
You must use showmanship and drama."

Use gimmicks and tricks to get the electorate's attention.
Communicate in a way that reaches all your voters.
Tie your campaign's themes together.
Do not just offer novel positions on new issues.
Tie new ideas with comfortable, familiar concepts.
Every campaign must amplify a single, clear message.

When you are unknown, you must create excitement.
If you are better known, you must still be interesting.
You must educate your supporters so they understand what to do
and say.

5 You inspire action in supporters by generating emotion.
You must also be able to control your own emotions.

At the start of a campaign, all volunteers are energetic.
As the campaign wears on, energy fades.
When it is time to vote, most supporters are tired.
You must use your volunteers wisely.
Avoid burning them out too early in the campaign.
You want their energy to increase as the election approaches.
This is how you master the energy of an electorate.

¹⁰Use discipline to await the chaos of battle.

Keep relaxed to await a crisis.

This is how you master emotion.

¹³Stay close to home to await a distant enemy.

Stay comfortable to await the weary enemy.

Stay well fed to await the hungry enemy.

This is how you master power.

Don't entice the enemy when his ranks are orderly. 6

You must not attack when his formations are solid.

This is how you master adaptation.

⁴You must follow these military rules.

Do not take a position facing the high ground.

Do not oppose those with their backs to the wall.

Do not follow those who pretend to flee.

Do not attack the enemy's strongest men.

Do not swallow the enemy's bait.

Do not block an army that is heading home.

Leave an escape outlet for a surrounded army.

Do not press a desperate foe.

This is how you use military skills.

EMOTION:

Strategy teaches that emotion is the key to action. If you control emotions, you control actions.

♦ ♦ ♦

When problems arise in a campaign, do not overreact.
Keep calm in the inevitable crisis.
This is how you master your own emotions.

Stay close to your constituents and see what new voters you attract.
Stay positive and wait for opponents to get tired.
Keep fund-raising and wait for other campaigns to feel the pinch.
This is how you master power.

6 Do not go after voter segments where the opposition is strong.
You must not campaign where others' constituents are solid.
This is how you master adapting.

You must follow these campaign rules:
Do not take a position on issues against strong prejudices.
Do not complain about those who are needy or in trouble.
Do not follow candidates who have failed.
Do not target your opponents' strongest issues.
Do not believe everything that opinion polls tell you.
Do not make it difficult for voters to support you.
Give the electorate options.
Do not make supporters feel pressured.
These are the rules of campaigning.

◆ ◆ ◆

MESSAGE:

Your message must not be how great you or your positions are, but how you can make voters great.

Related Articles from *Sun Tzu's Playbook*

In chapter seven, Sun Tzu teaches us to focus on building positions instead of on tearing down opponents. To learn the step-by-step techniques involved, we recommend the Sun Tzu's Warrior's Playbook *articles listed below.*

1.2.1 Competitive Landscapes: the arenas in which rivals jockey for position.

1.3.1 Competitive Comparison: competition as the comparison of positions.

1.5 Competing Agents: characteristics of competitors.

1.7 Competitive Power: the sources of superiority in challenges.

1.8.1 Creation and Destruction: the creation and destruction of competitive positions.

1.9 Competition and Production: the two opposing skill sets of competition and production.

2.1.3 Strategic Deception: misinformation and disinformation in competition.

2.6 Knowledge Leverage: getting competitive value out of knowledge.

2.7 Information Secrecy: the role of secrecy in relationships.

3.1 Strategic Economics: balancing the cost and benefits of positioning.

3.1.1 Resource Limitations: the inherent limitation of strategic resources.

3.1.3 Conflict Cost : the costly nature of resolving competitive comparisons by conflict.

3.1.6 Time Limitations: understanding the time limits on opportunities.

3.7 Defining the Ground: redefining a competitive arena to create relative mismatches.

4.7 Competitive Weakness: how certain opportunities can bring out our weaknesses.

6.1.2 Prioritizing Conditions: parsing complex competitive conditions into simple responses.

6.8 Competitive Psychology: improving competitive psychology even in adversity and failure.

7.4 Competitive Timing: the role of timing in creating momentum.

7.6 Productive Competition: using momentum to produce more resources.

7.6.2 Ground Creation: the creation of new competitive ground to be successful.

8.5 Leveraging Emotions: how we use emotion to obtain rewards.

9.5.2 Avoiding Emotion: the danger of exploiting environmental vulnerabilities for purely emotion reasons.

Chapter 8

Adaptability: Campaign Adjustments

Campaigners must continually address new situations that arise in the campaign process. The topic of this chapter is the need to continually change your approach based upon changing conditions. In Sun Tzu's view, successful campaign strategies must be dynamic.

Elections require surmounting certain specific challenges. In the chapter's first section, Sun Tzu lists situations (covered in greater detail in several other chapters) that show the need to constantly change your plans.

What looks like a voter objection is often the source of a campaign advantage. The next short section makes the point that you can be creative and constantly adapt your methods without being inconsistent in your results.

You should know your own weaknesses in politics, but you must adjust to the weaknesses of your competitors and the needs of your voters to campaign successfully. The third section, also short, explains that you can use the dynamics of competitive situations to influence the behavior of others.

It is the voter's job to come up with objections. In the fourth section, Sun Tzu covers the need to address the unpredictability of opponents in planning the defense of your position.

All political professionals have weaknesses. In the final section, Sun Tzu lists the five weaknesses of leaders and explains how you can defend against them in yourself and use them in others.

Adaptability

SUN TZU SAID:

Everyone uses the arts of war. 1
As a general, you get your orders from the government.
You gather your troops.
On dangerous ground, you must not camp.
Where the roads intersect, you must join your allies.
When an area is cut off, you must not delay in it.
When you are surrounded, you must scheme.
In a life-or-death situation, you must fight.
There are roads that you must not take.
There are armies that you must not fight.
There are strongholds that you must not attack.
There are positions that you must not defend.
There are government commands that must
not be obeyed.

ADAPTABILITY:

*Adaptability
doesn't mean
doing what you
want. It means
knowing the
appropriate
response to the
situation.*

14Military leaders must be experts in knowing
how to adapt to find an advantage.
This will teach you the use of war.

Campaign Adjustments

THE CAMPAIGNER HEARS:

1 Everyone uses the art of campaigning.
You decide to run at the behest of your supporters.
You then put together your campaign.
When the race is too risky, you must not run.
When you share goals, you must find partners.
When a constituency alienates most voters, you must not win it.
When all positions on an issue are taken, you must get creative.
In a do-or-die situation, you invest all your resources.
There are issues you should not chase.
There are endorsements you don't want.
There are voter groups you cannot win.
There are positions you must not defend.
There are times when you must ignore standard party policy.

RESILIENCE:

You must work to become an expert at knowing how to adapt to win an election.
This teaches you to leverage political comparisons.

You become more resilient when you see that no situation is good or bad in itself. All that matters is your response.

[16]Some commanders are not open to making adjustments to find an advantage.
They can know the shape of the terrain.
Still, they cannot find an advantageous position.

[19]Some military commanders do not know how to adjust their methods.
They can find an advantageous position.
Still, they cannot use their men effectively.

You must be creative in your planning. **2**
You must adapt to your opportunities and weaknesses.
You can use a variety of approaches and still have a consistent result.
You must adjust to a variety of problems and consistently solve them.

You can deter your potential enemy by using his **3** weaknesses against him.
You can keep your potential enemy's army busy by giving it work to do.
You can rush your potential enemy by offering him an advantageous position.

PLANNING:

Planning does not mean creating a rigid to-do list, but constantly rethinking what the situation demands.

Some campaigners are not open to making changes to fit a given electoral situation.

They might know what their voters think.

Still, they are unable to identify the positions on issues that win.

Some politicians attempt to campaign without adapting their usual methods.

They can figure out what the winning positions are.

Still, they cannot communicate those positions to the electorate.

2 You must be inventive in plotting your campaign.

You must change it to fit where voters are open and opponents weak.

You can use different approaches and still have predictable results. Every election offers unique challenges, but you can consistently find a good solution.

3 You can discourage potential opponents by using their weaknesses against them.

You can keep potential opponents' campaigns busy by giving them issues to address.

You can rush opponents into mistakes by offering them what looks like a good position.

CHANGE:

Winners embrace change because they can respond more quickly than their opponents.

You must make use of war. 4
Do not trust that the enemy isn't coming.
Trust your readiness to meet him by remaining patient.
Do not trust that the enemy won't attack.
Rely only on your ability to pick a place that the enemy can't
attack.

You can exploit five different faults in a leader. 5
If he is willing to die, you can kill him.
If he wants to survive, you can capture him.
He may have a quick temper.
You can then provoke him with insults.
If he has a delicate sense of honor, you can disgrace him.
If he loves his people, you can create problems for him.
In every situation, look for these five weaknesses.
They are common faults in commanders.
They always lead to military disaster.

[11]To overturn an army, you must kill its general.
To do this, you must use these five weaknesses.
You must always look for them.

PREPARATION:

*The battlefield
always favors
those who are
the most men-
tally prepared
for things not
going according
to plan.*

4 You must make use of political comparisons.
Do not trust that opponents will ignore an issue.
Instead, prepare yourself to compete on issues by keeping calm.
Do not trust that opponents won't attack your positions on issues.
Instead, rely on your ability to pick positions that opponents
cannot criticize.

5 Candidates can have five different character flaws.
If they are willing to lose elections, they will lose them.
If they want to ride it out, you can catch them.
They may get angry at criticism.
You can then provoke them with criticism.
If they always want to look good, you can embarrass them.
If they love their supporters, you can find flaws in those supporters.
In every situation, look for these five weaknesses.
They are common faults in candidates.
They can lead to disaster in elections.

To defeat a campaign, you must expose its candidate.
Know how to exploit these five weaknesses.
You must always be aware of them.

♦ ♦ ♦

FLAWS:

People naturally resist change, but if you are going to conquer your flaws, you have to change continually.

Related Articles from *Sun Tzu's Playbook*

In chapter eight, Sun Tzu teaches us the need to constantly adapt to the situation. To learn the step-by-step techniques involved, we recommend the Sun Tzu's Warrior's Playbook *articles listed below.*

1.8 Progress Cycle: the adaptive loop by which positions are advanced.

1.8.1 Creation and Destruction: the creation and destruction of competitive positions.

1.8.2 The Adaptive Loop: the continual reiteration of position analysis.

1.8.3 Cycle Time: the importance of speed in feedback and reaction.

1.8.4 Probabilistic Process: the role of chance in strategic processes and systems.

4.7.1 Command Weaknesses: the character flaws of leaders and how to exploit them.

5.2.1 Choosing Adaptability: choosing actions that allow us a maximum of future flexibility.

5.2.2 Campaign Methods: the use of campaigns and their methods.

5.2.3 Unplanned Steps: distinguishing campaign adjustments from steps in a plan.

5.3 Reaction Time: the use of speed in choosing actions.

5.3.1 Speed and Quickness: the use of pace within a dynamic environment.

6.0 Situation Response: selecting the actions most appropriate to a situation.

6.1 Situation Recognition: situation recognition in making advances.

6.1.1 Conditioned Reflexes: how we develop automatic, instantaneous responses.

6.1.2 Prioritizing Conditions: parsing complex competitive conditions into simple responses.

6.2 Campaign Evaluation: how we justify continued investment in an ongoing campaign.

6.2.1 Campaign Flow: seeing campaigns as a series of situations that flow logically from one to another.

6.2.2 Campaign Goals: assessing the value of a campaign by a larger mission.

6.3 Campaign Patterns: how knowing campaign stages gives us insight into our situation.

6.5 Nine Responses: the best responses to the nine common competitive situations.

6.7 Tailoring to Conditions: overcoming opposition using conditions in the environment.

6.7.1 Form Adjustments: adapting our responses based on the form of the ground.

6.7.2 Size Adjustments: adapting responses based on the relative size of opposing forces.

6.7.3 Strength Adjustments: how to adapt responses based on the relative strength of opposing missions.

Chapter 9

Armed March: Moving the Campaign Forward

The chapter's first section covers four different types of competitive "terrain" and how to navigate them. This means adapting your methods to the type of organizations or voting blocs with which you are dealing.

In the second section, Sun Tzu then briefly addresses the need to control the high ground in whatever type of situation you encounter. This relates to the methods and philosophy of interaction with your supporters.

The third section warns about the seasonal and hidden dangers inherent in exploring new territory. A campaigner must expect an overreaction to common temporary changes in conditions.

In the chapter's fourth section, the focus changes to understanding how your competitors might be changing the environment. This section explains various signs in the environment and how to interpret them in terms of competitors' activities.

In the long fifth section, Sun Tzu explains in detail how you can determine the condition and intentions of your opponents by interpreting their behavior.

Sun Tzu ends the chapter by describing how to know when you have gone as far as you can go in a new competitive arena and how you can regroup by growing your base of supporters. If there is no growth, eventually a campaign becomes too weak to win elections and it dies.

Armed March

Anyone moving an army must adjust to the enemy. 1
When caught in the mountains, rely on their valleys.
Position yourself on the heights facing the sun.
To win your battles, never attack uphill.
This is how you position your army in the mountains.

⁶When water blocks you, keep far away from it.
Let the invader cross the river and wait for him.
Do not meet him in midstream.
Wait for him to get half his forces across and
then take advantage of the situation.

¹⁰You need to be able to fight.
You can't do that if you are caught in water
when you meet an invader.
Position yourself upstream, facing the sun.
Never face against the current.
Always position your army upstream when
near the water.

TERRAIN:

*Strategy teaches
that all terrains
have different
forms and these
forms dictate
how you must
respond.*

Moving the Campaign Forward

THE CAMPAIGNER HEARS:

1 To move the campaign forward, adjust to where the voters are.
Within large, well-organized voting blocs, rely on the broad base.
Work up the hierarchy and become better known.
To win the group, never attack the group's leaders.
This is how you work within large, well-organized voter groups.

When the issues for a group are changing, stay away from them.
Let your opponents waste time on these shifting issues.
Don't compete on issues by changing your position.
Wait for them to get bogged down in these groups and
then use their shifting positions against them.

You need to be able to invest resources in a position.
You cannot do that if you are shifting positions on
issues when you are campaigning.

VOTERS:

Promote change and publicize that position.
Never stand against change.
Always position with the future among a changing
group of voters.

*Voters can fall
into four general
categories. They
can be difficult,
fluid, uncertain,
or flat.*

15You may have to move across marshes.
Move through them quickly without stopping.
You may meet the enemy in the middle of a marsh.
You must keep on the water grasses.
Keep your back to a clump of trees.
This is how you position your army in a marsh.

21On a level plateau, take a position that you can change.
Keep the higher ground on your right and to the rear.
Keep danger in front of you and safety behind.
This is how you position yourself on a level plateau.

25You can find an advantage in all four of these situations.
Learn from the great emperor who used positioning to
conquer his four rivals.

Armies are stronger on high ground and weaker on low. 2
They are better camping on sunny southern hillsides than
on shady northern ones.
Provide for your army's health and place men correctly.
Your army will be free from disease.
Done correctly, this means victory.

6You must sometimes defend on a hill or riverbank.
You must keep on the south side in the sun.
Keep the uphill slope at your right rear.

9This will give the advantage to your army.
It will always give you a position of strength.

With some groups, you have to deal with murky, uncertain issues.
Move quickly through these issues without taking a firm position.
You may have to face your opponents on the basis of these issues.
You must take a stand on the clearest aspects of these issues.
Base your position on what will prevent you from being blind-sided.
This is how you take positions on murky, uncertain issues.

Among easy-to-understand voter groups, offer flexible policies.
Base your positions on higher values, protecting your back.
See where the dangers are and base your position on what is safe.
This is how you position among easy-to-understand groups.

You can find opportunities in all types of voter groups.
Successful campaigners position themselves on issues to beat their competition.

2 Broad values are stronger and narrower ones are weaker.
It is better to stake out optimistic, sunny positions rather than vague, colder ones.
Provide for success and help supporters understand the issues.
Your campaign must be free of cynicism.
Do this correctly and you will win campaigns.

You must sometimes defend your position on a difficult issue.
Make the value of your policy obvious to others.
Base your position on higher, traditional values.

This will create opportunities for your campaign.
It will always help you unite your supporters.

Stop the march when the rain swells the river into rapids. 3
You may want to ford the river.
Wait until it subsides.

4All regions can have seasonal mountain streams that can
cut you off.
There are seasonal lakes.
There are seasonal blockages.
There are seasonal jungles.
There are seasonal floods.
There are seasonal fissures.
Get away from all these quickly.
Do not get close to them.
Keep them at a distance.
Maneuver the enemy close to them.
Position yourself facing these dangers.
Push the enemy back into them.

16Danger can hide on your army's flank.
There are reservoirs and lakes.
There are reeds and thickets.
There are mountain woods.
Their dense vegetation provides a hiding
place.
You must cautiously search through them.
They can always hide an ambush.

SEASONS:

*The changing
climate part of
every strategic
position means
that positions
continually
change.*

3 Stop campaigning when events roil change into chaos.
You may want to leverage the trends of change.
Wait until events calm down.

All campaigns and parties have temporary issues that can create obstacles.
There are temporary economic changes.
There are temporary negative media reports.
There are temporary legal issues.
There are temporary scheduling conflicts.
There are temporary holes in positioning.
Get past these situations quickly.
Do not get wrapped up in them.
Put them behind you.
Let your opponents get embroiled in them.
Keep your eye on these problems.
Push your opponents into them.

Problems can hide in your campaign's positions.
Beware of habits and prejudices.
Beware of unspoken assumptions.
Beware of unrevealed endorsements.
Uncommitted people can provide a secret base for political attack.
You must carefully research the electorate.
You do not want to be surprised.

PATIENCE:

Organizational changes endanger campaigns only if you rush into them without being aware of them.

Sometimes, the enemy is close by but remains calm. 4
Expect to find him in a natural stronghold.
Other times he remains at a distance but provokes battle.
He wants you to attack him.

5He sometimes shifts the position of his camp.
He is looking for an advantageous position.

7The trees in the forest move.
Expect that the enemy is coming.
The tall grasses obstruct your view.
Be suspicious.

11The birds take flight.
Expect that the enemy is hiding.
Animals startle.
Expect an ambush.

COMPETITORS:

If you cannot get information directly from competitors, you can get it by observing the environment.

15Notice the dust.
It sometimes rises high in a straight line.
Vehicles are coming.
The dust appears low in a wide band.
Foot soldiers are coming.
The dust seems scattered in different areas.
The enemy is collecting firewood.
Any dust is light and settling down.
The enemy is setting up camp.

4 An opponent runs in your election but is quiet.
You should expect that he has a strong position.
Another opponent distances her position from yours.
She plans to attack your position.

An opponent's position on an issue seems to invite attack.
Always expect that he has a secret advantage.

Polls in the election begin to shift.
Expect that an opponent is active.
The election is difficult to evaluate.
Expect to be surprised once you are in it.

Your mutual contacts may suddenly become shy.
Suspect that the competition plans a surprise.
Your supporters may become uncertain.
The opposition is ambushing you.

EVALUATION:

Opponents don't tell you what they are planning, so you must judge them by what you see in the field.

Listen to rumors from the street.
Sometimes rumors are clear and aimed at you.
You are being targeted.
Rumors can appear broadly in the area.
This means that opponents have many feet on the street.
The news is scattered among different groups.
Opponents are conducting political research.
News of the opposition becomes rarer and rarer.
This means that they are waiting.

Your enemy speaks humbly while building up forces. 5
He is planning to advance.

3The enemy talks aggressively and pushes as if to advance.
He is planning to retreat.

5Small vehicles exit his camp first.
They move the army's flanks.
They are forming a battle line.

8Your enemy tries to sue for peace but without offering a
treaty.
He is plotting.

10Your enemy's men run to leave and yet form ranks.
You should expect action.

12Half his army advances and the other half retreats.
He is luring you.

14Your enemy plans to fight but his men just stand there.
They are starving.

16Those who draw water drink it first.
They are thirsty.

18Your enemy sees an advantage but does not advance.
His men are tired.

5 Opponents cry "underdog" while amassing supporters.
Expect them to increase pressure.

Your opponents contest every issue and employ smear tactics.
They are close to giving up.

Endorsers move out into the electorate.
They contact undecided voter groups.
They are targeting their segments.

Your opponents seem to agree with you on an issue without offering a clear position.
Expect a trap.

Opponents seem to drop from the race but keep organizing.
Expect them to return.

Potential opponents send mixed signals about challenging you.
They want you to make the first move.

Opponents stay in the race but their supporters aren't canvassing.
They have exhausted their volunteers.

Your opponents send repeated appeals for "any amount."
They are out of money.

Your opponents have a clear opportunity but do nothing.
They are demoralized.

²⁰Birds gather.
Your enemy has abandoned his camp.

²²Your enemy's soldiers call in the night.
They are afraid.

²⁴Your enemy's army is raucous.
The men do not take their commander
seriously.

JUDGMENT:

*You best judge
your competi-
tors' situation by
what they and
their supporters
do rather than
what they say.*

²⁶Your enemy's banners and flags shift.
Order is breaking down.

²⁸Your enemy's officers are irritable.
They are exhausted.

³⁰Your enemy's men kill their horses for meat.
They are out of provisions.

³²They don't put their pots away or return to their tents.
They are desperate.

³⁴Enemy troops appear sincere and agreeable.
But their men are slow to speak to each other.
They are no longer united.

³⁷Your enemy offers too many incentives to his men.
He is in trouble.

Opposition endorsers come to you.
Your opponent has abandoned the election.

Opposition supporters make contact with you.
This means that they are afraid.

Opponents' volunteers are undisciplined.
This means that they are not taking organizers
seriously.

Opponents' teams and positions suddenly change.
This means that they are disorganized.

Opponents' organizers argue with each other.
They are getting weary.

> **PROBLEMS:**
>
> *In political competition, you need to take advantage of the problems that your opponents are having.*

Your opponents take money from atypical sources.
They are out of resources.

Opponents' supporters aren't having fun or getting any rest.
They are frantic.

Opposing campaign members seem sincere and dedicated, but
their workers speak poorly of their leaders.
They are no longer unified.

The opposition makes too many extravagant promises.
The campaign is in trouble.

39Your enemy gives out too many punishments.
His men are weary.

41Your enemy first acts violently and then is afraid of your
larger force.
His best troops have not arrived.

43Your enemy comes in a conciliatory manner.
He needs to rest and recuperate.

45Your enemy is angry and appears to welcome battle.
This goes on for a long time, but he doesn't attack.
He also doesn't leave the field.
You must watch him carefully.

If you are too weak to fight, you must find more men. 6
In this situation, you must not act aggressively.
You must unite your forces.
Prepare for the enemy.
Recruit men and stay where you are.

6You must be cautious about making plans
and adjust to the enemy.
You must gather more men.

EXPANSION:

Campaigns into new areas expand your control but they also spread your resources over a wider territory.

Opponents are trying to increase voters' fears.
Their supporters are wearing down.

An opposing campaign first criticizes your positions but then tries placate you.
Your opponent is expecting better campaign resources.

Another campaign tries to collaborate with you.
This means that it needs your help.

An opponent sounds aggressive and targets your supporters.
This goes on for a long time, but there is no attack.
She doesn't withdraw from the campaign.
In these situations, you must be cautious.

6 If you are too weak, you need more donors and volunteers.
In this situation, you must not aggressively campaign.
You must unite your supporters.
You must prepare them against the opposition.
Recruit more people and build up your resources.

You must not assume too much about the future
and adjust to shifts in the opposition.
You must develop new sources of support.

PAUSING:

Your campaign reaches its limit when resources are stretched too thin to allow you to win new voters.

With new, undedicated soldiers, you can depend on 7 them if you discipline them.
They will tend to disobey your orders.
If they do not obey your orders, they will be useless.

4You can depend on seasoned, dedicated soldiers.
But you must avoid disciplining them without reason.
Otherwise, you cannot use them.

7You must control your soldiers with esprit de corps.
You must bring them together by winning victories.
You must get them to believe in you.

10Make it easy for people to know what to do by training
your people.
Your people will then obey you.
If you do not make it easy for people to know
what to do, you won't train your people.
Then they will not obey.

14Make your commands easy to follow.
You must understand the way a crowd thinks.

YOUR TROOPS:

Your success depends totally on your ability to train, motivate, and manage the people with whom you work.

7 With new, inexperienced volunteers, you can use them if you are clear and firm.

Otherwise, your new volunteers will be confused.

If they are confused, they cannot help your campaign.

It is different with experienced campaign members.

You must show them your willingness to listen.

They serve you best by giving you new ideas.

You must control your volunteers through shared success.

You must unite them into a team by winning more supporters.

You must have confidence in your campaign.

Make it easy for your volunteers to know what to do by educating them.

They will then do what you need them to do.

If you make your political position too complex, you will not be able to train your volunteers.

They will stop listening to you.

You must make directions easy to understand.

You must understand how groups of people think.

SIMPLICITY:

The biggest part of your job as a campaigner is to make voters' decisions as easy as possible.

Related Articles from *Sun Tzu's Playbook*

In chapter nine, Sun Tzu discusses the basics of recognizing conditions in new territory. To learn the step-by-step techniques involved, we recommend the Sun Tzu's Warrior's Playbook *articles listed below.*

1.1.0 Position Paths: the continuity of strategic positions over time.

1.2.2 Exploiting Exploration: how competitive landscapes are searched and positions utilized.

2.1 Information Value: knowledge and communication as the basis of strategy.

2.1.1 Information Limits: making good decisions with limited information.

2.2.1 Personal Relationships: why information depends on personal relationships.

2.2.2 Mental Models: how mental models simplify decision-making.

2.2.3 Standard Terminology: how mental models must be shared to enable communication.

2.3 Personal Interactions: making progress through personal interactions.

2.3.1 Action and Reaction: how we advance based on how others react to our actions.

2.3.2 Reaction Unpredictability: why we can never exactly predict the reactions of others.

2.3.3 Likely Reactions: the range of potential reactions in gathering information.

2.3.4 Using Questions: using questions in gathering information and predicting reactions.

4.0 Leveraging Probability: making better decisions regarding our choice of opportunities.

4.3 Leveraging Form: how we can leverage the form of our territory.

4.3.1 Tilted Forms: opportunities that are dominated by uneven forces.

4.3.2 Fluid Forms: opportunities that are dominated by fast-changing directional forces.

4.3.3 Soft Forms: opportunities that are dominated by forces that create uncertainty.

4.3.4 Neutral Forms: opportunities where the terrain has no dominant forces.

4.4 Strategic Distance: relative proximity in strategic space.

4.4.1 Physical Distance: the issues of proximity in physical space.

4.4.2 Intellectual Distance: the challenges of moving through intellectual space.

Chapter 10

地 形

Field Position: Campaign Positions

For Sun Tzu, every position is a stepping stone to a better position. This chapter examines in detail six common types of positions. For the campaigner, these are analogous to positions on issues.

Sun Tzu begins the chapter with a detailed description of the six types of field positions and how to utilize them. Understanding the campaign's relative position on the issues is paramount.

The second section lists the six flaws in campaign teams and how to diagnose them. Each of these six flaws arises in and is amplified by the specific field position. Sun Tzu points to the commander, or leader, as the source of these weaknesses.

In the third section, Sun Tzu examines the situations that you must consider in moving from one temporary position to another. He further cautions against letting ego push you into making unwise or untimely comparisons.

There is a connection between caring for supporters and insisting that they make decisions. In the fourth section, Sun Tzu addresses the proper way of providing leadership to people as you usher them into new situations.

As always, your ability to campaign with confidence depends on your knowledge. In the final section, Sun Tzu addresses the need to compare your relative field position with that of your opponent before choosing a course of action.

Field Position

SUN TZU SAID:

Some field positions are unobstructed. 1
Some field positions are entangling.
Some field positions are supporting.
Some field positions are constricted.
Some field positions give you a barricade.
Some field positions are spread out.

7You can attack from some positions easily.
Other forces can meet you easily as well.
We call these unobstructed positions.
These positions are open.
In them, be the first to occupy a high, sunny
area.
Put yourself where you can defend your
supply routes.
Then you will have an advantage.

IN THE FIELD:

*Strategy teaches
that you can
learn the true
nature of a
territory only
once you have
entered into it.*

Campaign Positions

THE CAMPAIGNER HEARS:

1 Some positions on issues are open.
Some positions on issues are entangling.
Some positions on issues are ideal.
Some positions on issues are exclusive.
Some positions on issues create barriers.
Some positions on issues are too broad.

You can advance from some positions easily.
Political opponents can counter you easily as well.
These positions on issues are open.
They are open for debate.
In them, be the first to offer an optimistic, clever solution.
Your position on these issues should generate financial support.
Then you will have an opportunity.

OPPORTUNITY:

There are six different types of positions on issues and each requires the appropriate approach.

[14]You can attack from some positions easily.
Disaster arises when you try to return to them.
These are entangling positions.
These field positions are one-sided.
Wait until your enemy is unprepared.
You can then attack from these positions and win.
Avoid a well-prepared enemy.
You will try to attack and lose.
Since you can't return, you will meet disaster.
These field positions offer no advantage.

[24]You cannot leave some positions without losing an
advantage.
If the enemy leaves this ground, he also loses an advantage.
We call these supporting field positions.
These positions strengthen you.
The enemy may try to entice you away.
Still, hold your position.
You must entice the enemy to leave.
You then strike him as he is leaving.
These field positions offer an advantage.

[33]Some field positions are constricted.
Get to these positions first.
You must fill these areas and await the enemy.
Sometimes, the enemy will reach them first.
If he fills them, do not follow him.
However, if he fails to fill them, you can go after him.

You can expand easily from positions on some issues.
You cannot return to them if your expansion fails.
These positions on issues are entangling.
You can expand their appeal but not refocus them again.
Wait until you can certainly win broader voter support.
You can use these issues as a basis for your success.
Avoid diluting these issues for groups you cannot win.
Your advances will then fail.
Since you cannot refocus, you will lose supporters.
Positions on these issues are a problem.

You cannot improve on some positions without losing broad support.
Your opponents cannot improve on them either.
These are ideal positions on issues.
These positions win elections.
You may be tempted to try to change them.
You must keep them in place.
Encourage your opponents to offer alternative positions.
You can then attack them for being stupid.
These positions offer a clear advantage.

Some positions on issues are exclusive.
You must adopt them before your opponents do.
You must defend them and await a challenge.
Your opponents may use these positions first.
If their positions are solid, don't try to challenge them.
However, if their positions have holes, you can go after them.

39Some field positions give you a barricade.
Get to these positions first.
You must occupy their southern, sunny heights in order to
await the enemy.
Sometimes the enemy occupies these areas first.
If so, entice him away.
Never go after him.

45Some field positions are too spread out.
Your force may seem equal to the enemy.
Still you will lose if you provoke a battle.
If you fight, you will not have any advantage.

49These are the six types of field positions.
Each battleground has its own rules.
As a commander, you must know where to go.
You must examine each position closely.

Some armies can be outmaneuvered. 2
Some armies are too lax.
Some armies fall down.
Some armies fall apart.
Some armies are disorganized.
Some armies must retreat.

YOUR FORCES:

*The term
"forces" means
all elements
used against the
competition,
both personnel
and resources.*

7Know all six of these weaknesses.
They create weak timing and disastrous
positions.
They all arise from the army's commander.

Some positions on issues create protective barriers.
You must establish these positions before opponents do.
You then must promote your position and encourage opposition challenges.
Sometimes opponents establish these positions first.
If so, wait for your opponents to change their position.
Never challenge these positions directly.

Some positions on issues are too broad.
Positions that appeal to everyone only seem strong.
Still, they lose when compared to more focused positions.
Investing in these positions is not an opportunity.

These are the six types of positions on issues.
Each election has its own voter groups and issues.
As a campaigner, you must know who your voters are.
You must examine your potential positions closely.

2 Some campaigns can be outmaneuvered.
Some campaigns are stagnant.
Some campaigns stumble.
Some campaigns self-destruct.
Some campaigns are chaotic.
Some campaigns must reorganize.

You must recognize these six weaknesses.
They put you out of synch and create losing positions.
Your decisions create them.

CHARACTER:

Flaws in leaders come from excesses of courage, analysis, discipline, trustworthiness, and caring.

10One general can command a force equal to the enemy.
Still his enemy outflanks him.
This means that his army can be outmaneuvered.

13Another can have strong soldiers but weak officers.
This means that his army is too lax.

15Another has strong officers but weak soldiers.
This means that his army will fall down.

17Another has subcommanders that are angry and defiant.
They attack the enemy and fight their own battles.
The commander cannot know the battlefield.
This means that his army will fall apart.

21Another general is weak and easygoing.
He fails to make his orders clear.
His officers and men lack direction.
This shows in his military formations.
This means that his army is disorganized.

COMMAND:

*Only one person
makes the key
decisions in an
organization,
thereby shaping
it and creating
any flaws.*

26Another general fails to predict the enemy.
He pits his small forces against larger ones.
His weak forces attack stronger ones.
He fails to pick his fights correctly.
This means that his army must retreat.

Some politicians may have as many resources as their opposition.
Still, their opponents blindside them.
This means their campaigns can be outmaneuvered.

Other campaigns have strong supporters but weak organizers.
Their campaigns are stagnant.

Other campaigns have strong organizers but weak supporters.
Their campaigns will stumble.

Other campaigns have organizers that are angry and defiant.
They attack opponents based on their own agendas.
These campaigns cannot know their true priorities.
These campaigns will self-destruct.

Some campaigns are lazy and sloppy.
They fail to make their priorities clear.
Their organizers and supporters lack direction.
This shows in the campaign's lack of focus.
These campaigns are chaotic.

Some candidates fail to foresee opposing moves.
They pit small voter segments against larger ones.
They pit poor positions against better ones.
They fail to pick their issues correctly.
Their campaigns must reorganize.

BALANCE:

A campaign must balance positioning, communication, message, focus, and competitive thinking.

³¹You must know all about these six weaknesses.
You must understand the philosophies that lead to defeat.
When a general arrives, you can know what he will do.
You must study each general carefully.

You must control your field position. 3
It will always strengthen your army.

³You must predict the enemy to overpower him and win.
You must analyze the obstacles, dangers, and distances.
This is the best way to command.

⁶Understand your field position before you meet opponents.
Then you will succeed.
You can fail to understand your field position and meet opponents.
Then you will fail.

¹⁰You must provoke battle when you will certainly win.
It doesn't matter what you are ordered.
The government may order you not to fight.
Despite that, you must always fight when you will win.

FORESIGHT:

Once you can quickly diagnose a situation, you know the appropriate response when others leave openings.

¹⁴Sometimes provoking a battle will lead to a loss.
The government may order you to fight.
Despite that, you must avoid battle when you will lose.

You must understand all six campaign weaknesses.
You must understand the decisions that lead to these failures.
When candidates run, you can predict their decisions.
You must study each candidate carefully.

3 You must control your positions on issues.
It will always strengthen your campaign.

You must foresee how to discredit the opponent's alternatives.
You must see the voters' difficulties, problems, and needs.
This is the best way to win elections.

Know your positions before comparing them to opponents'.
If you do, you will always win the election.
You may not understand your positions before comparing them to opponents'.
You will fail.

You challenge opponents when you are certain to win comparisons.
It doesn't matter what others are saying.
Your political party may tell you not to invest resources.
Still, you must always invest resources when votes can be won.

Sometimes inviting a comparison will lead to a loss.
Your political party may take a certain position.
Despite that, you must avoid issues where you will lose.

FLEXIBILITY:

As you learn more about your situation, you must be willing to adapt your plans accordingly.

[17]You must advance without desiring praise.

You must retreat without fearing shame.

The only correct move is to preserve your troops.

This is how you serve your country.

This is how you reward your nation.

Think of your soldiers as little children. 4

You can make them follow you into a deep river.

Treat them as your beloved children.

You can lead them all to their deaths.

[5]Some leaders are generous but cannot use their men.

They love their men but cannot command them.

Their men are unruly and disorganized.

These leaders create spoiled children.

Their soldiers are useless.

You may know what your soldiers will do in an attack. 5

You may not know if the enemy is vulnerable to attack.

You will then win only half the time.

You may know that the enemy is vulnerable to attack.

You may not know if your men have the capability of
attacking him.

You will still win only half the time.

You may know that the enemy is vulnerable to attack.

You may know that your men are ready to attack.

You may not, however, know how to position yourself in the
field for battle.

You will still win only half the time.

You must never campaign to satisfy your ego.
You must avoid issues without embarrassment.
The only right move is to keep your supporters.
This is how you serve your political party.
This is how you make your campaign successful.

4 Think of your campaign workers as your family.
They will support you in difficult circumstances.
Train them with care and understanding.
They will support you faithfully.

Some candidates are great but they cannot organize their campaign.
They love their people but do not guide them.
Their supporters are unhappy and confused.
These campaigners create disgruntled supporters.
Their support is useless.

5 You may know what issues to use when canvassing voters.
You may not know if your opponents are vulnerable on those issues.
If you don't, you have done only part of your job.
You may know if your opponents are vulnerable on your issues.
You may not know that your campaign workers can make a winning presentation.
If you don't, you have done only part of your job.
You may know if your opponents are vulnerable on your issues.
You may know that your workers can make a winning presentation.
You may not know how to position your campaign in the voter segments you need.
If you don't, you have done only part of your job.

[11]You must know how to make war.
You can then act without confusion.
You can attempt anything.

[14]We say:
Know the enemy and know yourself.
Your victory will be painless.
Know the weather and the field.
Your victory will be complete.

♦ ♦ ♦

RELATIVITY:

Strategically, all your qualities, both good and bad, arise only in comparison with your opponents.

You must truly understand political choices.
You can then act with certainty.
You can campaign for any office.

Pay attention:
Know your opponents and know your campaign.
Then elections are effortless.
Understand voters' feelings and voter groups.
Then your success is assured.

✦ ✦ ✦

SYNTHESIS:

Your knowledge of positions, opponents, issues, and voters' needs combine to create a campaign.

Related Articles from *Sun Tzu's Playbook*

In chapter ten, Sun Tzu discusses the use of temporary positions in building relationships with voters. To learn the step-by-step techniques involved, we recommend the Sun Tzu's Warrior's Playbook *articles listed below.*

2.3 Personal Interactions: making progress through personal interactions.

2.3.1 Action and Reaction: how we advance based on how others reaction to our actions.

2.3.2 Reaction Unpredictability: why we can never exactly predict the react of others.

2.3.3 Likely Reactions: the range of potential reactions in gathering information.

2.3.4 Using Questions: using questions in gathering information and predicting reactions.

4.5 Opportunity Surfaces: judging potential opportunities from a distance.

4.5.1 Surface Area: choosing opportunities on the basis of their size.

4.5.2 Surface Barriers: how to select opportunities by evaluating obstacles.

4.5.3 Surface Holding Power: sticky and slippery situations.

4.6 Six Benchmarks: simplifying the comparisons of opportunities.

Chapter 11

九地

Types of Terrain: Campaign Stages

As a political campaign moves forward, it passes through nine common situations or stages. Each of these stages poses a specific type of challenge that requires a specific response. The key to moving forward quickly is instantly recognizing and reacting to these situations as they arise. Since speed is essential, campaigners train themselves and their workers to instantly recognize these situations and to respond by reflex using strategility.

In these stages, the earliest steps are usually the easiest and you have the most options. As you make progress, the challenges from opposition get more difficult. You have fewer and fewer options until the final stages, which are the most difficult and desperate.

The increasing difficulty of a campaign over time makes sense because each step forward takes you further toward victory. You are winning more and more of those your opponents hoped were "their" voters. Opponents push back harder against you. At the beginning, you are relatively close to voters you know and your only challenge is defending against larger opponents. As you move further and further into new voter groups, more and more challenges arise.

Through the entire process, you must maintain the pace of progress. Good leaders learn how to use the increasing pressure from political competition to unite and focus their positions. The psychological pressures of political changes can destroy an organization if a leader doesn't immediately know how to respond.

Types of Terrain

GROUND:

Ground, territory, and terrain are all from the same Chinese concept, "di," which also means situation and condition.

SUN TZU SAID:

Use the art of war. 1
Know when the terrain will scatter you.
Know when the terrain is easy.
Know when the terrain is disputed.
Know when the terrain is open.
Know when the terrain is intersecting.
Know when the terrain is dangerous.
Know when the terrain is bad.
Know when the terrain is confined.
Know when the terrain is deadly.

11Warring parties must sometimes fight
inside their own territory.
This is scattering terrain.

13When you enter hostile territory, your penetration is shallow.
This is easy terrain.

15Some terrain gives you an advantageous position.
But it gives others an advantageous position as well.
This will be disputed terrain.

Campaign Stages

THE CAMPAIGNER HEARS:

1 Use your ability to compare.
Know when the campaign stage is tenuous.
Know when the campaign stage is easy.
Know when the campaign stage is contentious.
Know when the campaign stage is open.
Know when the campaign stage is shared.
Know when the campaign stage is serious.
Know when the campaign stage is difficult.
Know when the campaign stage is limited.
Know when the campaign stage is do-or-die.

STAGES:

The nine stages described here explain a logical evolution that campaigns go through as they progress.

You must sometimes defend against a new opponent when you are the incumbent.
This is the tenuous stage of the campaign.

When you've recently entered a race, your campaign is still a novelty and little known.
This is the easy stage of the campaign.

Some changes in political climate give you an opportunity.
But they give your opposition an opportunity as well.
This is the contentious stage of the campaign.

18You can use some terrain to advance easily.
Others can advance along with you.
This is open terrain.

21Everyone shares access to a given area.
The first one to arrive there can gather a larger group than anyone else.
This is intersecting terrain.

24You can penetrate deeply into hostile territory.
Then many hostile cities are behind you.
This is dangerous terrain.

27There are mountain forests.
There are dangerous obstructions.
There are reservoirs.
Everyone confronts these obstacles on a campaign.
They make bad terrain.

32In some areas, the entry passage is narrow.
You are closed in as you try to get out of them.
In this type of area, a few people can effectively attack your much larger force.
This is confined terrain.

36You can sometimes survive only if you fight quickly.
You will die if you delay.
This is deadly terrain.

Sometimes, you can make easy progress in your campaign.
New opponents, however, can still come in at any time.
This is the open stage of the campaign.

Every candidate shares access to the same undecided voters.
The first campaign to develop a sizable following will dominate the race.
This is the shared stage of the campaign.

You can start winning over initially hostile voter groups.
But you still have many critics within those groups.
This is the serious stage of the campaign.

There are party hierarchies to satisfy.
There are legal restrictions on campaigning.
There are limits on donations.
All campaigners meet these challenges in a campaign.
This is the difficult stage of the campaign.

In some campaigns, there is a key transition point.
You have only a very limited number of options.
Your campaign is vulnerable to the loss of a few key supporters, endorsers, or donors.
This is the limited stage of the campaign.

Sometimes you succeed only if you commit all your resources.
The campaign will fail if you delay.
This is the do-or-die stage of the campaign.

[39]To be successful, you must control scattering terrain by avoiding battle.

Control easy terrain by not stopping.

Control disputed terrain by not attacking.

Control open terrain by staying with the enemy's forces.

Control intersecting terrain by uniting with your allies.

Control dangerous terrain by plundering.

Control bad terrain by keeping on the move.

Control confined terrain by using surprise.

Control deadly terrain by fighting.

Go to an area that is known to be good for waging war. **2**
Use it to cut off the enemy's contact between his front and back lines.

Prevent his small parties from relying on his larger force.

Stop his strong divisions from rescuing his weak ones.

Prevent his officers from getting their men together.

Chase his soldiers apart to stop them from amassing.

Harass them to prevent their ranks from forming.

[8]When joining battle gives you an advantage, you must do it.
When it isn't to your benefit, you must avoid it.

CONTROL:

Each of the nine "terrains," "conditions," or "stages" demands a specific form of response.

[10]A daring soldier may ask:
"A large, organized enemy army and its general are coming.
What do I do to prepare for them?"

To be successful, control the tenuous stage by rising above the challenge.

During the easy stage, do not slow down your advance.

During the contentious stage, avoid political showdowns.

In the open stage, stay even with political rivals.

In the shared stage, make good alliances.

In the serious stage, concentrate on fund-raising.

In the difficult stage, work through the problems.

In the limited stage, get creative.

In the do-or-die stage, push through to the win.

2 Find the voter groups to which you have the most appeal.

Use those voter groups as wedges to divide opponents' supporters and donors.

Prevent opponents' small groups from joining into larger groups.

Keep their good positions from overshadowing their weaker ones.

Stop their organizers from gathering supporters from these groups.

Identify opposing campaign workers and keep them apart.

Prevent the opposition from getting organized.

When you have the advantage, force voters to decide.

When you do not have an advantage, delay their decisions.

You wonder:

"A well-organized opponent is moving into my political territory.

What should I do?"

DECISION:

Voters make their decisions not only on election day, but throughout the course of the campaign.

¹³Tell him:

"First seize an area that the enemy must have.
Then he will pay attention to you.
Mastering speed is the essence of war.
Take advantage of a large enemy's inability to keep up.
Use a philosophy of avoiding difficult situations.
Attack the area where he doesn't expect you."

You must use the philosophy of an invader. 3
Invade deeply and then concentrate your forces.
This controls your men without oppressing them.

⁴Get your supplies from the riches of the territory.
They are sufficient to supply your whole army.

⁶Take care of your men and do not overtax them.
Your esprit de corps increases your momentum.
Keep your army moving and plan for surprises.
Make it difficult for the enemy to count your forces.
Position your men where there is no place to run.
They will then face death without fleeing.
They will find a way to survive.
Your officers and men will fight to their utmost.

¹⁴Military officers who are committed lose their fear.
When they have nowhere to run, they must stand firm.
Deep in enemy territory, they are captives.
Since they cannot escape, they will fight.

Pay attention.
Raise issues that opponents must address quickly.
You can then guide them.
Urgency is the essence of camaigns.
Take advantage of a leading candidate's inability to keep up.
Act without hesitation.
Keep the discussion where the competition is unprepared.

3 You must make a deep impression on the electorate.
Penetrate opposition voters and plant your volunteers among them.
Give your supporters the job of contacting those they understand.

Do your fund-raising among donors who support your party.
They have the money you need to fund your campaign.

Take care of your campaign workers and do not overburden them.
Their enthusiasm increases your political momentum.
Keep your campaign active in the community and expect surprises.
Make it difficult to know how much support you have.
Position your campaign so your workers have no good alternatives.
They will stay with you even when problems arise.
They will find a way to defend you.
Your organizers and supporters will invest everything they can.

Political organizers who are committed lose their uncertainty.
When they have no good alternatives, they will stay with you.
Get their personal pledges to your campaign to hold them.
Since they are personally committed, they will focus.

[18]Commit your men completely.
Without being posted, they will be on guard.
Without being asked, they will get what is needed.
Without being forced, they will be dedicated.
Without being given orders, they can be trusted.

[23]Stop them from guessing by removing all their doubts.
Stop them from dying by giving them no place to run.

[25]Your officers may not be rich.
Nevertheless, they still desire plunder.
They may die young.
Nevertheless, they still want to live forever.

[29]You must order the time of attack.
Officers and men may sit and weep until their lapels are wet.
When they stand up, tears may stream down their cheeks.
Put them in a position where they cannot run.
They will show the greatest courage under fire.

Make good use of war. 4
This demands instant reflexes.
You must develop these instant reflexes.
Act like an ordinary mountain snake.
If people strike your head then stop them with your tail.
If they strike your tail then stop them with your head.
If they strike your middle then use both your head and tail.

All your workers should be completely committed to winning.
Without being warned, everyone must be on guard.
Without being asked, everyone must tell you what is needed.
Without being forced, everyone must do what needs to be done.
Without being told, everyone must trust that they know what to do.

Stop any second-guessing by making assignments clear.
Avoid failure by leaving your people no excuses.

Your organizers may not be politically successful.
This is not because they do not desire political success.
They may lose the election.
Nevertheless, they will still want to succeed eventually.

You must set deadlines for contacting voters quickly.
People will complain that they cannot meet the deadlines.
When they must do it, they still will tell you that they cannot.
Put them in a position where they have no choice.
They will find a way to get the work done.

4 Make good use of position comparison.
You must respond to criticisms immediately.
Your responses should be prepared and rehearsed.
You must be able to act on instinct.
If your intentions are challenged, you win by discussing results.
If the results are questioned, you win by discussing intentions.
If your processes are criticized, win with intentions and results.

[8]A daring soldier asks:

"Can any army imitate these instant reflexes?"

We answer: "It can."

[12]To command and get the most out of proud people, you must study adversity.

People work together when they are in the same boat during a storm.

In this situation, one rescues the other just as the right hand helps the left.

[15]Use adversity correctly.

Tether your horses and bury your wagons' wheels.

ADVERSITY:

Strategically, unity is strength, and nothing unites a force more than being threatened by a common enemy.

Still, you can't depend on this alone.

An organized force is braver than lone individuals.

This is the art of organization.

Put the tough and weak together.

You must also use the terrain.

[22]Make good use of war.

Unite your men as one.

Never let them give up.

The commander must be a military professional. 5

This requires confidence and detachment.

You must maintain dignity and order.

You must control what your men see and hear.

They must follow you without knowing your plans.

You may question these reflexes.
Can you prepare political responses?
There is only one answer: You must!

To guide and influence civic leaders, you must understand how to use the pressure of unexpected events.
You must bond with civic leaders by seeing their problems as your problems.
In the face of challenges, they will work together with you when they realize that you want to help.

Share the worries of the voters you want to win.
Tie your future together with theirs by putting yourself at risk.
Even this is not enough.
An organized campaign is braver than lone individuals.
This is the art of giving people a voice.
Join the outspoken with the quiet.
You must also use political issues.

LEADERSHIP:

You position yourself for political leadership when your thinking focuses on your voters' concerns.

Make good use of political comparison.
Make it easy for volunteers to join you.
Make it hard for campaign workers to leave.

5 You must take the lead in campaign decisions.
This requires confidence and detachment.
You must maintain your leadership and focus.
You must control what your campaign workers see and hear.
They must believe without your explaining all the details.

[6]You can reinvent your men's roles.

You can change your plans.

You can use your men without their understanding.

[9]You must shift your campgrounds.

You must take detours from the ordinary routes.

You must use your men without giving them your strategy.

[12]A commander provides what is needed now.

This is like climbing high and being willing to kick away your ladder.

You must be able to lead your men deep into different surrounding territory.

And yet, you can discover the opportunity to win.

[16]You must drive men like a flock of sheep.

You must drive them to march.

You must drive them to attack.

You must never let them know where you are headed.

You must unite them into a great army.

You must then drive them against all opposition.

This is the job of a true commander.

[23]You must adapt to the different terrain.

You must adapt to find an advantage.

You must manage your people's affections.

You must study all these skills.

You must reinvent your campaign workers' roles.
You can change your focus on different voting blocs.
You can only lead if you know more than everyone else.

You must change your established positions.
You must offer new ways to get the work done.
You must guide campaign workers without making excuses.

Your decisions must address exactly what is needed at the moment.
You must be willing to go out on a limb and take a risk to win an election.
You must get deeply involved with your voters to uncover their true needs.
These desires create the opportunities you need to win them over.

You must inspire campaign workers to identify as a special group.
You must get out canvassing voters.
You must show your workers how to advance your positions.
You must constantly stimulate them with what is coming next.
You must unite supporters into a great force of campaign workers.
You must motivate these campaign workers against your opponents.
This is the job of a true campaigner.

You must adjust at every campaign stage.
You must adjust your positions on issues to win voters.
You must excite your supporters' emotions.
You can learn all these skills.

Always use the philosophy of invasion. 6
Deep invasions concentrate your forces.
Shallow invasions scatter your forces.
When you leave your country and cross the border, you must take control.
This is always critical ground.
You can sometimes move in any direction.
This is always intersecting ground.
You can penetrate deeply into a territory.
This is always dangerous ground.
You penetrate only a little way.
This is always easy ground.
Your retreat is closed and the path ahead tight.
This is always confined ground.
There is sometimes no place to run.
This is always deadly ground.

[16]To use scattering terrain correctly, you must inspire your men's devotion.
On easy terrain, you must keep in close communication.
On disputed terrain, you try to hamper the enemy's progress.
On open terrain, you must carefully defend your chosen position.
On intersecting terrain, you must solidify your alliances.
On dangerous terrain, you must ensure your food supplies.
On bad terrain, you must keep advancing along the road.
On confined terrain, you must stop information leaks from your headquarters.
On deadly terrain, you must show what you can do by killing the enemy.

6 Always go after the undecided voters.
Winning the opposition's voters focuses your campaign.
Weak commitment dissipates your supporters.
At the beginning of a commitment to winning a voter group, you must take the lead.
This is a critical time.
Your political interests often coincide with those of others.
You must create healthy partnerships.
You can invest everything in the campaign for an office.
This is always the serious stage.
All political races look promising when you first start in them.
This is always the easy part of the campaign.
A campaign can narrow until you must rely on a few key resources.
This is the limited stage of the campaign.
A campaign can narrow to one issue alone.
This is the do-or-die stage.

To succeed in the tenuous stage, you must have your supporters' devotion.
In the easy stage, you must contact as many voters as possible.
In the contentious stage, you must create problems for opponents.
In the open stage, you must defend your established positions.
In the shared stage, you must join your partners.
In the serious stage, you must raise funds.
In the difficult stage, you must keep the campaign going.
In the limited stage, you must keep your limitations a secret from those who don't need to know.
In the do-or-die stage, you must prove yourself by winning your election.

25Make your men feel like an army.

Surround them and they will defend themselves.

If they cannot avoid it, they will fight.

If they are under pressure, they will obey.

Do the right thing when you don't know your 7
different enemies' plans.

Don't attempt to meet them.

3You don't know the position of mountain forests, dangerous
obstructions, and reservoirs?

Then you cannot march the army.

You don't have local guides?

You won't get any of the benefits of the terrain.

7There are many factors in war.

You may lack knowledge of any one of them.

If so, it is wrong to take a nation into war.

10You must be able to control your government's war.

If you divide a big nation, it will be unable to put together a
large force.

KNOWLEDGE:

Strategy teaches that you can replace investment of time and effort with more complete information.

Increase your enemy's fear of your ability.

Prevent his forces from getting together and
organizing.

Make campaign workers feel powerful.

Put them out among voters, and they will succeed.

When they have no choice, they will invest all their efforts.

When they are asked to do more, they will follow your lead.

7 Do the right thing when you do not understand your opponents' positions.

Do not try to compare your positions to theirs.

You do not understand the electorate's voting habits, opinions, and needs?

Then you cannot start a political campaign.

You don't know experienced local politicians?

You will not know your voters' thinking or needs.

There is so much to know in campaigning.

You do not want to miss anything.

Otherwise, you cannot control the campaign.

You must be able to use your political party's local organizers.

If you can divide the opposing party's support, they will not be able to win a majority.

Make your opponents afraid to run against you.

Prevent opponents' supporters from uniting and organizing.

REEVALUATE:

Analysis must be repeated constantly as you reexamine the five key factors that define your positions.

¹⁴Do the right thing and do not arrange outside alliances
before their time.
You will not have to assert your authority prematurely.
Trust only yourself and your self-interest.
This increases the enemy's fear of you.
You can make one of his allies withdraw.
His whole nation can fall.

²⁰Distribute rewards without worrying about having a system.
Halt without the government's command.
Attack with the whole strength of your army.
Use your army as if it were a single man.

²⁴Attack with skill.
Do not discuss it.
Attack when you have an advantage.
Do not talk about the dangers.
When you can launch your army into deadly ground, even if
it stumbles, it can still survive.
You can be weakened in a deadly battle and yet be stronger
afterward.

³⁰Even a large force can fall into misfortune.
If you fall behind, however, you can still turn defeat into victory.
You must use the skills of war.
To survive, you must adapt yourself to your enemy's purpose.
You must stay with him no matter where he goes.
It may take a thousand miles to kill the general.
If you correctly understand him, you can find the skill to do it.

Do the right thing and do not depend on political alliances before you are ready.

Then you will not have to fight for control of the campaign.

Trust yourself and your own instincts.

This increases the potential opposition's respect for you.

You can convince the potential allies of opponents to abandon them.

Their whole party may then collapse.

Promise political favors without worrying about working it out.

Stop without your party's instruction.

Advance your cause with the force of your campaign.

Use your campaign workers as a united force.

Campaign with skill.

Do not just talk about it.

Be aggressive when you find an edge.

Do not advertise the risks.

You can go through difficult stages and lose voters, but you can still win.

You may lose ground in one voter segment, but you can also learn from your mistakes.

You can succeed many times and still get into bad situations.

If you make mistakes, you can turn initial failure into success.

You must use your campaigning skills.

You must adapt completely to the election's conditions.

You must stay with your voters no matter where they go.

You can turn voters around and overtake the leading candidate.

If you understand voters' options, you can find ways to win them.

Manage your government correctly at the start of a war. 8
Close your borders and tear up passports.
Block the passage of envoys.
Encourage the halls of power to rise to the occasion.
You must use any means to put an end to politics.
Your enemy's people will leave you an opening.
You must instantly invade through it.

[8]Immediately seize a place that they love.
Do it quickly.
Trample any border to pursue the enemy.
Use your judgment about when to fight.

[12]Doing the right thing at the start of war is like
approaching a woman.
Your enemy's men must open the door.
After that, you should act like a streaking rabbit.
The enemy will be unable to catch you.

✦ ✦ ✦

BEGINNINGS:

*The start of a
campaign is a
delicate time
when you set the
direction for the
entire course of
the campaign.*

8 Manage local party people correctly at the start of a campaign.
Tie them to you and keep others from winning their support.
Stop them from looking for other potential candidates.
Get their complete commitment to your campaign.
You must do everything you can to unite your party behind you.
Your opponents' supporters will create opportunities for you.
Quickly take advantage of these weaknesses.

Quickly win the support of a voter group that your party loves.
Waste no time.
Avoid going through party channels to win them.
Use your best judgment about where to compete.

Success at the beginning of an election comes from wooing your voters like you would woo a lover.
Your potential opponents will eventually neglect them.
When they do, you should act quickly.
Never let your opponents catch up with you.

OPENINGS:

*You cannot win
an election
without the
cooperation of
opponents who
leave you the
opening that you
need.*

Related Articles from *Sun Tzu's Playbook*

In chapter eleven, Sun Tzu explains situation response. To learn the step-by-step methods used, we recommend the Sun Tzu's Warrior's Playbook *articles listed below.*

6.0 Situation Response: selecting the actions most appropriate to a situation.

6.1 Situation Recognition: situation recognition in making advances.

6.1.1 Conditioned Reflexes: how we develop automatic, instantaneous responses.

6.1.2 Prioritizing Conditions: parsing complex competitive conditions into simple responses.

6.2 Campaign Evaluation: how we justify continued investment in an ongoing campaign.

6.2.1 Campaign Flow: seeing campaigns as a series of situations that flow logically from one to another.

6.2.2 Campaign Goals: assessing the value of a campaign by a larger mission.

6.3 Campaign Patterns: how knowing campaign stages gives us insight into our situation.

6.3.1 Early-Stage Situations: the common situations that arise the earliest in campaigns.

6.3.2 Middle-Stage Situations: how progress creates transitional situations in campaigns.

6.3.3 Late-Stage Situations: understanding the final and most dangerous stages of campaigns.

6.4 Nine Situations: the nine common competitive situations.

6.4.1 Dissipating Situations: situations where defensive unity is destroyed.

6.4.2 Easy Situations: recognizing situations of easy initial progress.

6.4.3 Contentious Situations: identifying situations that invite conflict.

6.4.4 Open Situations: recognizing situations that are races without a course.

6.4.5 Intersecting Situations: recognizing situations that bring people together.

6.4.6 Serious Situations: identifying situations where resources can be cut off.

6.4.7 Difficult Situations: recognizing situations where serious barriers must be overcome.

6.4.8 Limited Situations: identifying situations defined by a bottleneck.

6.4.9 Desperate Situations: identifying situations where destruction is possible.

6.5 Nine Responses: using the best responses to the nine common competitive situations.

6.5.1 Dissipating Response: responding to dissipation by the use of offense as defense.

6.5.2 Easy Response: responding to easy situations by overcoming complacency.

6.5.3 Contentious Response: responding to contentious situations by knowing how to avoid conflict.

6.5.4 Open Response: responding to open situations by keeping up with the opposition.

6.5.5 Intersecting Response: the formation of situational alliances.

6.5.6 Serious Response: responding to serious situations by finding immediate income.

6.5.7 Difficult Response: the role of persistence in responding to difficult situations.

6.5.8 Limited Response: the need for secret speed in limited situations.

6.5.9 Desperate Response: using all our resources in responding to desperate situations.

6.6 Campaign Pause: knowing when to stop advancing a position.

6.8 Competitive Psychology: improving competitive psychology even in adversity and failure.

6.8.1 Adversity and Creativity: how we use adversity to spark our creativity.

6.8.2 Strength in Adversity: using adversity to increase a group's unity and focus.

Chapter 12

Attacking With Fire: Firestorms of Controversy

For the campaigner, the lessons in this chapter offer an outline for leveraging factors in the environment to directly impact your opponent's standing in the race. In this chapter, we talk about using an indirect type of attack, social pressure. Social pressure means getting others—the news media, special interest groups, even government agencies, to act on your behalf. Your campaigns can use information to spark these attacks and follow up on them, but you do not engage in them directly. Various outside "social forces" create a "firestorm" around a campaign.

Sun Tzu begins by describing the five specific targets for these attacks from the environment. We use these five targets to discuss various social forces that might come into play.

The second section in this chapter emphasizes that the social pressure itself is less important than the response to it.

In the third section, Sun Tzu briefly compares using fire and water. Water is Sun Tzu's general metaphor for change that is a part of climate.

The "firestorm" of controversy is all about emotion. Sun Tzu ends his discussion of fire and desire by addressing the need to control emotional responses in both undertaking and responding to attacks.

Though this chapter is commonly translated in terms of offensive attack, the original Chinese can also be read as a prescription for defense against these attacks.

Attacking With Fire

FIRE:

Classical strategy describes the element of fire as a weapon and uses it as a metaphor for all weapons.

SUN TZU SAID:

There are five ways of attacking with fire. 1
The first is burning troops.
The second is burning supplies.
The third is burning supply transport.
The fourth is burning storehouses.
The fifth is burning camps.

7To make fire, you must have the resources.
To build a fire, you must prepare the raw materials.

9To attack with fire, you must be in the right season.
To start a fire, you must have the time.

11Choose the right season.
The weather must be dry.

13Choose the right day.
Pick a season when the grass is as high as the side of a cart.

15Choose the right time of day.
You want days when the wind rises in the morning.

Firestorms of Controversy

THE CAMPAIGNER HEARS:

1 There are five ways to create firestorms of controversy:
The first is using the media to raise personal shortcomings.
The second is inspiring legal action to consume money.
The third is using special interest groups.
The fourth is using past associates to raise questions.
The fifth is using pundits to attack past political associations.

To create a controversy, you must know your opponents' history.
To work it, you must have the raw details of information that excite interest.

To make it into a firestorm, you must pick the right time.
To ignite it, you must work patiently behind the scenes.

Choose the period in the campaign.
There must be a dry spell on election news.

Choose the right day.
Pick a time when news will reach voters while they are deciding.

Choose the right moment to strike.
Wait until other news favors you or hurts your opponent.

Everyone attacks with fire. 2

You must create five different situations with fire and be able to adjust to them.

3You start a fire inside the enemy's camp.
Then attack the enemy's periphery.

5You launch a fire attack, but the enemy remains calm.
Wait and do not attack.

7The fire reaches its height.
Follow its path if you can.
If you can't follow it, stay where you are.

REACTION:

The environment is unpredictable so you must always act based upon how situations develop rather than your plans.

10Spreading fires on the outside of camp can kill.
You can't always get fire inside the enemy's camp.
Take your time in spreading it.

13Set the fire when the wind is at your back.
Don't attack into the wind.
Daytime winds last a long time.
Night winds fade quickly.

17Every army must know how to adjust to the five possible attacks by fire.
Use many men to guard against them.

2 All politics uses social pressure.
You can use five different situations of social pressure and adapt to them.

Social trends can undermine the image of the campaign's party.
Then you attack the campaign's issues on the basis of that image.

Social news raises an issue, but opponents don't rise to the bait.
Wait until they do.

Social outcry mounts to a peak.
Leverage the issues that it creates if you can.
If you can't use these issues, stay out of the controversy.

CONTROL:

The less control you have over the way others react, the more control you must have over the way you react.

The news creates a lot of damaging stories sur-rounding a party.
You can't always apply every story directly to an opponent's campaign.
Don't worry; over time it will do damage.

If you spark a controversy, don't get caught in it.
Don't spark controversies that come back to you.
Well publicized stories last a long time.
Hushed up stories fade quickly.

Every campaign must know how to deal with these five social attacks.
Use your supporters to track rumors about your campaign.

When you use fire to assist your attacks, you are clever. 3
Water can add force to an attack.
You can also use water to disrupt an enemy's forces.
It does not, however, take his resources.

You win in battle by getting the opportunity to attack. 4
It is dangerous if you fail to study how to accomplish this
achievement.
As commander, you cannot waste your opportunities.

4We say:
A wise leader plans success.
A good general studies it.
If there is little to be gained, don't act.
If there is little to win, do not use your men.
If there is no danger, don't fight.

10As the leader, you cannot let your anger interfere with the
success of your forces.
As commander, you cannot let yourself
become enraged before you go to battle.
Join the battle only when it is in your
advantage to act.
If there is no advantage in joining a battle,
stay put.

DECISION:

*Your decisions
must use the
emotions of
others. Your
emotions cannot
determine your
decisions.*

3 When you campaign using social forces, you are smart.

Social changes can add force to this pressure.

You can also use social changes to confuse an opponent's supporters.

However, change alone cannot completely destroy political positions.

4 You can win an election by getting an opportunity to use social pressure.

It is dangerous not to study how social forces work in an election.

In elections, you cannot afford to waste your efforts.

Pay attention!

A wise candidate expects to win.

A good campaigner studies how.

If a move won't win votes, don't use it.

If it won't win many votes, don't use your campaign workers.

If you are safe from danger, don't invest your resources.

You must never let your ego interfere with advancing your campaign.

As a campaigner, you must never become emotional when you confront your opponent.

Do not engage opponents unless you can outshine them.

If there is no benefit in engaging opponents, don't get involved.

SUCCESS:

A great position is not one that wins you applause. It is one that advances your political career.

¹⁴Anger can change back into happiness.
Rage can change back into joy.
A nation once destroyed cannot be brought back to life.
Dead men do not return to the living.

¹⁸This fact must make a wise leader cautious.
A good general is on guard.

²⁰Your philosophy must be to keep the nation peaceful and
the army intact.

EMOTION:

*Emotional grati-
fication is never
the goal of a
competition. You
must never lose
sight of your
goals in the heat
of battle.*

Your feelings are temporary.
Events that first make you angry can become a source of joy.
A campaign once destroyed cannot be brought back to life.
Completely disgraced candidates cannot get elected.

Knowing this, you must be careful in using social pressure.
You must always guard against these social attacks.

Your plan must keep your campaign healthy and your supporters
behind you.

◆ ◆ ◆

THE PAYOFF:

Controversy, like
all weapons,
cuts both ways.
Playing to hot
topics can be
exciting, but
it can also be
dangerous.

Related Articles from *Sun Tzu's Playbook*

In chapter twelve, Sun Tzu discusses the use of environmental weapons. To learn the step-by-step techniques involved, we recommend the Sun Tzu's Warrior's Playbook *articles listed below.*

9.0 Understanding Vulnerability: the use of common environmental attacks.

9.1 Climate Vulnerability: our vulnerability to environmental crises arising from change.

9.1.1 Climate Rivals: how changing conditions create opponents.

9.1.2 Threat Development: how changing conditions create environmental threats.

9.2 Points of Vulnerability: our points of vulnerability during an environmental crisis.

9.2.1 Personnel Risk: the vulnerability of key individuals.

9.2.2 Immediate Resource Risk: the vulnerability of the resources required for immediate use.

9.2.3 Transportation/Communication Risk: how firestorms choke normal channels of movement and communication.

9.2.4 Asset Risk: the threats to our fixed assets.

9.2.5 Organizational Risk: targeting the roles and responsibilities within an organization.

9.3 Crisis Leadership: maintaining the support of our supporters during attacks.

Chapter 13

用 間

Using Spies: Political Intelligence

While the Chinese is translated as "spies" in this chapter, its actual meaning from Sun Tzu is "information channels." As a campaigner, you need to know how to gather information. In his final chapter, Sun Tzu addresses what he considers to be the most important element of strategy: political intelligence.

Not getting the right information in the campaign process is extremely expensive. Sun Tzu begins by describing the many costs, both to a campaign and society, that can be minimized by the right information. He makes the point that this information must come from people as sources.

You need a wide spectrum of information to run a campaign. In the second section, Sun Tzu discusses the different dimensions to that information.

There are rules for using intelligence in politics. The third section of this chapter discusses techniques for evaluating information and managing information sources.

In elections, it is often the details that matter. This chapter's fourth section teaches that before you tackle a specific problem you must first find sources that provide a complete picture of that problem.

The past is the key to your political future. The closing section points out that the history of competition shows that success depends first on the cultivation of good information sources. For campaigners, this means knowing how to know what is needed.

Using Spies

SUN TZU SAID:

All successful armies require thousands of men. 1
They invade and march thousands of miles.
Whole families are destroyed.
Other families must be heavily taxed.
Every day, a large amount of money must be spent.

6Internal and external events force people to move.
They are unable to work while on the road.
They are unable to find and hold a useful job.
This affects 70 percent of thousands of families.

10You can watch and guard for years.
Then a single battle can determine victory in a
day.
Despite this, bureaucrats worship the value of
their salary money too dearly.
They remain ignorant of the enemy's
condition.
The result is cruel.

ECONOMICS:

*The science of
strategy is based
on the idea that
better informa-
tion can be used
to eliminate
other costs.*

Political Intelligence

THE CAMPAIGNER HEARS:

1 All successful campaigns require many supporters.
They have to get out and contact thousands of voters.
The families of campaign workers are disrupted.
The families of donors give heavily to the campaign.
Every day of your campaign, you're spending money.

Bad local and national political decisions force citizens to move.
People "vote with their feet," going elsewhere to find work.
Bad politics increases the number of unemployed.
Politics affects 70 percent of the national economy.

You can watch and guard your values for years.
Then a single judge's decision can change all the rules
in a day.
Despite this, entrenched incumbents worship the
value of their position too dearly.
People cannot afford to stay ignorant of the government's condition.
The result is cruel.

INTELLIGENCE:

Voters are always dependent on politicians who have the best information about government issues.

[15]They are not leaders of men.
They are not servants of the state.
They are not masters of victory.

[18]You need a creative leader and a worthy commander.
You must move your troops to the right places to beat others.
You must accomplish your attack and escape unharmed.
This requires foreknowledge.
You can obtain foreknowledge.
You can't get it from demons or spirits.
You can't see it from professional experience.
You can't check it with analysis.
You can only get it from other people.
You must always know the enemy's situation.

You must use five types of spies. 2
You need local spies.
You need inside spies.
You need double agents.
You need doomed spies.
You need surviving spies.

NETWORKS:

The key to gathering useful information is to have a range of different types of sources in your network.

[7]You need all five types of spies.
No one must discover your methods.
You will then be able to put together a true picture.
This is the commander's most valuable resource.

Foolish politicians do not lead.
They are not the servants of the people.
They do not command and control success.

You must be an intelligent, valuable leader.
You must move supporters to the right issues to beat opponents.
You must damage opposing positions without hurting yourself.
This requires information.
You can get this information.
You won't get it from psychology.
You won't get it from past experience.
You can't reason it out.
You can only get it by asking questions of people.
You must always know your opposition's situation.

2 You must use five types of political intelligence.
You need information on voter demographics.
You need information on opponents' positions.
You need information on winnable allies.
You need information from unfriendly critics.
You need information from contacts in the community.

You must use all five types of sources.
If you do, no one can challenge your knowledge.
You can put the facts into a complete picture of the situation.
This perspective is the politician's most valuable resource.

INDIVIDUALS:

You need to build personal relationships to get the intelligence that makes a competitive difference.

¹¹You need local spies.
Get them by hiring people from the countryside.

¹³You need inside spies.
Win them by subverting government officials.

¹⁵You need double agents.
Discover enemy agents and convert them.

¹⁷You need doomed spies.
Deceive professionals into being captured.
Let them know your orders.
They then take those orders to your enemy.

²¹You need surviving spies.
Someone must return with a report.

Your job is to build a complete army. 3
No relations are as intimate as the ones with spies.
No rewards are too generous for spies.
No work is as secret as that of spies.

⁵If you aren't clever and wise, you can't use spies.
If you aren't fair and just, you can't use spies.
If you can't see the small subtleties, you won't get the truth
from spies.

⁸Pay attention to small, trifling details!
Spies are helpful in every area.

You need voter demographics.
Get them by acquiring the history past voting patterns.

You need information on opponents' positions.
Get it by making friends inside opposing campaigns.

You must recruit winnable allies.
Discover opponents' key supporters and win them over.

You need unfriendly critics.
Deceive them into making statements that hurt their credibility.
Let them think they know your positions.
They then take those false positions to your opponents.

You must have contacts in the community.
They must let you know what is happening in the streets.

3 Your job is to win a well-rounded group of supporters.
No relationships are as critical as those with good sources.
No price is too high to pay for good information.
Good information must be kept secret.

You must be perceptive to see the patterns in data.
You must be open and unbiased to evaluate information.
If you are not sensitive to subtleties, you will not find the truth in
the data.

Pay attention to the smallest details.
Intelligence sources make campaigning easy.

[10]Spies are the first to hear information, so they must not spread information.

Spies who give your location or talk to others must be killed along with those to whom they have talked.

You may want to attack an army's position. **4**
You may want to attack a certain fortification.
You may want to kill people in a certain place.
You must first know the guarding general.
You must know his left and right flanks.
You must know his hierarchy.
You must know the way in.
You must know where different people are stationed.
You must demand this information from your spies.

[10]You want to know the enemy spies in order to convert them into your men.
You must find sources of information and bribe them.
You must bring them in with you.
You must obtain them as double agents and use them as your emissaries.

SPECIFICS:

*The more spe-
cific your targets
become, the
more specific
the information
needed to win
them.*

Your sources are closest to the action; they should keep you informed but not spread information.

Sources who reveal your plans and knowledge must be cut off; block them and all their contacts.

4 You may want to approach an opponent's voter bloc.
You may want to go after specific issue.
You may want to contact certain key people.
You must first know who the key people are.
You must know their assistants.
You must know their organization.
You must know how to reach them.
You must know who influences their decisions.
You must get this information from your sources.

You must know how to get close to the key people within the opponent's campaign.
You must find sources and give them the attention they want.
You must get close to them.
You must win them as secret supporters and use them as your ambassadors.

INSIDERS:

Your goal is to get inside the information loop used by your opponents or key voter groups.

[14]Do this correctly and carefully.
You can contact both local and inside spies and obtain their
support.
Do this correctly and carefully.
You create doomed spies by deceiving professionals.
You can use them to give false information.
Do this correctly and carefully.
You must have surviving spies capable of bringing you
information at the right time.

[21]These are the five different types of intelligence work.
You must be certain to master them all.
You must be certain to create double agents.
You cannot afford to be too cost conscious in creating these
double agents.

This technique created the success of ancient Shang. 5
This is how the Shang held their dynasty.

[3]You must always be careful of your success.
Learn from Lu Ya of Shang.

[5]Be a smart commander and a good general.
You do this by using your best and brightest people for spying.
This is how you achieve the greatest success.
This is how you meet the necessities of war.
The whole army's position and ability to move depends on
these spies.

You must do this carefully.

You can contact both local media and opponents' supporters and obtain their support.

You must also do this carefully.

You cultivate unfriendly sources by feeding them information.

You can then feed them false information.

You must do this carefully and confidentially.

You must have contacts in the community that let you know when things are going well or badly.

There are five different types of political intelligence sources.

You must be certain to master them all.

You must win a few of the opposition's people.

You must not be too frugal with your time or money in gathering intelligence.

5 Intelligence sources were the source of all past political power. It is how political power is maintained.

You must be concerned about your own success.

Learn from the successes of the past.

You must be an informed and capable campaigner.

You must use your best and brightest people to gather information.

This is how you make the biggest gains.

This is how you meet your electorate's needs.

All your campaign's positions and your ability to advance depend on political intelligence.

Related Articles from *Sun Tzu's Playbook*

In his final chapter, Sun Tzu explains how to use information channels. To learn the step-by-step techniques involved, we recommend the Sun Tzu's Warrior's Playbook *articles listed below.*

2.0.0 Developing Perspective: adding depth to competitive analysis.

2.1 Information Value: knowledge and communication as the basis of strategy.

2.1.1 Information Limits: making good decisions with limited information.

2.1.3 Strategic Deception: misinformation and disinformation in competition.

2.1.4 Surprise: how the creation of surprise depends on the nature of information.

2.2 Information Gathering: gathering competitive information.

2.2.1 Personal Relationships: why information depends on personal relationships.

2.2.3 Standard Terminology: how mental models must be shared to enable communication.

2.3 Personal Interactions: making progress through personal interactions.

2.3.4 Using Questions: using questions in gathering information and predicting reactions.

2.3.5 Infinite Loops: predicting reactions on the basis of the "you-know-that-I-know-that-you-know" problem.

2.3.6 Promises and Threats: the use of promises and threats as strategic moves.

2.4 Contact Networks: the range of contacts needed to create perspective.

2.4.1 Ground Perspective: getting information on a new competitive arena.

2.4.2 Climate Perspective: getting perspective on temporary external conditions.

2.4.3 Command Perspective: developing sources for understanding decision-makers.

2.4.4 Methods Perspective: developing contacts who understand best practices.

2.4.5 Mission Perspective: how we develop and use a perspective on motivation.

2.5 The Big Picture: building big-picture strategic awareness.

2.6 Knowledge Leverage: getting competitive value out of knowledge.

2.7 Information Secrecy: defining the role of secrecy in relationships.

Glossary of Key Strategic Concepts

This glossary is keyed to the most common English words used in the translation of *The Art of War*. Those terms only capture the strategic concepts generally. Though translated as English nouns, verbs, adverbs, or adjectives, the Chinese characters on which they are based are totally conceptual, not parts of speech. For example, the character for CONFLICT is translated as the noun "conflict," as the verb "fight," and as the adjective "disputed." Ancient written Chinese was a conceptual language, not a spoken one. More like mathematical terms, these concepts are primarily defined by the strict structure of their relationships with other concepts. The Chinese names shown in parentheses with the characters are primarily based on Pinyin, but we occasionally use Cantonese terms to make each term unique.

ADVANCE (JEUN 進): to move into new GROUND; to expand your POSITION; to move forward in a campaign; the opposite of FLEE.

ADVANTAGE, *benefit* (LI 利): an opportunity arising from having a better POSITION relative to an ENEMY; an opening left by an ENEMY; a STRENGTH that matches against an ENEMY'S WEAKNESS; where fullness meets emptiness; a desirable characteristic of a strategic POSITION.

AIM, *vision, foresee* (JIAN 見): FOCUS on a specific ADVANTAGE, opening, or opportunity; predicting movements of an ENEMY; a skill of a LEADER in observing CLIMATE.

ANALYSIS, *plan* (GAI 計): a comparison of relative POSITION; the examination of the five factors that define a strategic POSITION; a combination of KNOWLEDGE and VISION; the ability to see through DECEPTION.

ARMY: see WAR.

ATTACK, *invade* (GONG 攻): a movement to new GROUND; advancing a strategic POSITION; action against an ENEMY in the sense of moving into his GROUND; opposite of DEFEND; does not necessarily mean CONFLICT.

BAD, *ruined* (PI 坯): a condition of the GROUND that makes ADVANCE difficult; destroyed; terrain that is broken and difficult to traverse; one of the nine situations or types of terrain.

BARRICADED: see OBSTACLES.

BATTLE (ZHAN 戰): to challenge; to engage an ENEMY; generically, to meet a challenge; to choose a confrontation with an ENEMY at a specific time and place; to focus all your resources on a task; to establish superiority in a POSITION; to challenge an ENEMY to increase CHAOS; that which is CONTROLLED by SURPRISE; one of the

four forms of ATTACK; the response to a DESPERATE SITUATION; character meaning was originally "big meeting," though later took on the meaning "big weapon"; not necessarily CONFLICT.

BRAVERY, *courage* (YONG 勇): the ability to face difficult choices; the character quality that deals with the changes of CLIMATE; courage of conviction; willingness to act on vision; one of the six characteristics of a leader.

BREAK, *broken, divided* (PO 破): to DIVIDE what is COMPLETE; the absence of a UNITING PHILOSOPHY; the opposite of UNITY.

CALCULATE, *count* (SHU 數): mathematical comparison of quantities and qualities; a measurement of DISTANCE or troop size.

CHANGE, *transform* (BIAN 變): transition from one CONDITION to another; the ability to adapt to different situations; a natural characteristic of CLIMATE.

CHAOS, *disorder* (JUAN 亂): CONDITIONS that cannot be FORESEEN; the natural state of confusion arising from BATTLE; one of six weaknesses of an organization; the opposite of CONTROL.

CLAIM, *position, form* (XING 形): to use the GROUND; a shape or specific condition of GROUND; the GROUND that you CONTROL; to use the benefits of the GROUND; the formations of troops; one of the four key skills in making progress.

CLIMATE, *heaven* (TIAN 天): the passage of time; the realm of uncontrollable CHANGE; divine providence; the weather; trends that CHANGE over time; generally, the future; what one must AIM at in the future; one of five key factors in ANALYSIS; the opposite of GROUND.

COMMAND (LING 令): to order or the act of ordering subordinates; the decisions of a LEADER; the creation of METHODS.

COMPETITION: see WAR.

COMPLETE: see UNITY.

CONDITION: see GROUND.

CONFINED, *surround* (WEI 圍): to encircle; a SITUATION or STAGE in which your options are limited; the proper tactic for dealing with an ENEMY that is ten times smaller; to seal off a smaller ENEMY; the characteristic of a STAGE in which a larger FORCE can be attacked by a smaller one; one of nine SITUATIONS or STAGES.

CONFLICT, *fight* (ZHENG 争): to contend; to dispute; direct confrontation of arms with an ENEMY; highly desirable GROUND that creates disputes; one of nine types of GROUND, terrain, or stages.

CONSTRICTED, *narrow* (AI 狹): a confined space or niche; one of six field positions; the limited extreme of the dimension distance; the opposite of SPREAD-OUT.

CONTROL, *govern* (CHI 治): to manage situations; to overcome disorder; the opposite of CHAOS.

DANGEROUS: see SERIOUS.

DANGERS, *adverse* (AK 阨): a condition that makes it difficult to ADVANCE; one of three dimensions used to evaluate advantages; the dimension with the extreme field POSITIONS of ENTANGLING and SUPPORTING.

DEATH, *desperate* (SI 死): to end or the end of life or efforts; an extreme situation in which the only option is BATTLE; one of nine STAGES or types of TERRAIN; one of five types of SPIES; opposite of SURVIVE.

DECEPTION, *bluffing, illusion* (GUI 詭): to control perceptions; to control information; to mislead an ENEMY; an attack on an opponent's AIM; the characteristic of war that confuses perceptions.

DEFEND (SHOU 守): to guard or to hold a GROUND; to remain in a POSITION; the opposite of **ATTACK.**

DETOUR (YU 迂): the indirect or unsuspected path to a POSITION; the more difficult path to ADVANTAGE; the route that is not DIRECT.

DIRECT, *straight* (JIK 直): a straight or obvious path to a goal; opposite of DETOUR.

DISTANCE, *distant* (YUAN 遠): the space separating GROUND; to be remote from the current location; to occupy POSITIONS that are not close to one another; one of six field positions; one of the three dimensions for evaluating opportunities; the emptiness of space.

DIVIDE, *separate* (FEN 分): to break apart a larger force; to separate from a larger group; the opposite of JOIN and FOCUS.

DOUBLE AGENT, *reverse* (FAN 反): to turn around in direction; to change a situation; to switch a person's allegiance; one of five types of spies.

EASY, *light* (QING 輕): to require little effort; a SITUATION that requires little effort; one of nine STAGES or types of terrain; opposite of SERIOUS.

EMOTION, *feeling* (XIN 心): an unthinking reaction to AIM, a necessary element to inspire MOVES; a component of esprit de corps; never a sufficient cause for ATTACK.

ENEMY, *competitor* (DIK 敵): one who makes the same CLAIM; one with a similar GOAL; one with whom comparisons of capabilities are made.

ENTANGLING, *hanging* (GUA 懸): a POSITION that cannot be returned to; any CONDITION that leaves no easy place to go; one of six field positions.

EVADE, *avoid* (BI 避): the tactic used by small competitors when facing large opponents.

FALL APART, *collapse* (BENG 崩): to fail to execute good decisions; to fail to use a CONSTRICTED POSITION; one of six weaknesses of an organization.

FALL DOWN, *sink* (HAAM 陷): to fail to make good decisions; to MOVE from a SUPPORTING POSITION; one of six weaknesses of organizations.

FEELINGS, *affection, love* (CHING 情): the bonds of relationship; the result of a shared PHILOSOPHY; requires management.

FIGHT, *struggle* (DOU 鬥): to engage in CONFLICT; to face difficulties.

FIRE (HUO 火): an environmental weapon; a universal analogy for all weapons.

FLEE, *retreat, northward* (BEI 北): to abandon a POSITION; to surrender GROUND; one of six weaknesses of an ARMY; opposite of ADVANCE.

FOCUS, *concentrate* (ZHUAN 專): to bring resources together at a given time; to UNITE forces for a purpose; an attribute of having a shared PHILOSOPHY; the opposite of *divide*.

FORCE (LEI 力): power in the simplest sense; a GROUP of people bound by UNITY and FOCUS; the relative balance of STRENGTH in opposition to WEAKNESS.

FORESEE: see AIM.

FULLNESS: see STRENGTH.

GENERAL: see LEADER.

GOAL: see PHILOSOPHY.

GROUND, *situation, stage* (DI 地): the earth; a specific place; a specific condition; the place one competes; the prize of competition; one of five key factors in competitive analysis; the opposite of CLIMATE.

GROUPS, *troops* (DUI 隊): a number of people united under a shared PHILOSOPHY; human resources of an organization; one of the five targets of fire attacks.

INSIDE, *internal* (NEI 内): within a TERRITORY or organization; an insider; one of five types of spies; opposite of OUTSIDE.

INTERSECTING, *highway* (QU 衢): a SITUATION or GROUND that allows you to JOIN; one of nine types of terrain.

JOIN (HAP 合): to unite; to make allies; to create a larger FORCE; opposite of DIVIDE.

KNOWLEDGE, *listening* (ZHI: 知): to have information; the result of listening; the first step in advancing a POSITION; the basis of strategy.

LAX, *loosen* (SHII 弛): too easygoing; lacking discipline; one of six weaknesses of an army.

LEADER, *general, commander* (JIANG 將): the decision-maker in a competitive unit; one who LISTENS and AIMS; one who manages TROOPS; superior of officers and men; one of the five key factors in analysis; the conceptual opposite of SYSTEM, the established methods, which do not require decisions.

LEARN, *compare* (XIAO 效): to evaluate the relative qualities of ENEMIES.

LISTEN, *obey* (TING 聽): to gather KNOWLEDGE; part of ANALYSIS.

LISTENING: see KNOWLEDGE.

LOCAL, *countryside* (XIANG 鄉): the nearby GROUND; to have KNOWLEDGE of a specific GROUND; one of five types of SPIES.

MARSH (ZE 澤): GROUND where footing is unstable; one of the four types of GROUND; analogy for uncertain situations.

METHOD: see SYSTEM.

MISSION: see PHILOSOPHY.

MOMENTUM, *influence* (SHI 勢): the FORCE created by SURPRISE set up by STANDARDS; used with TIMING.

MOUNTAINS, *hill, peak* (SHAN 山): uneven GROUND; one of four types of GROUND; an analogy for all unequal SITUATIONS.

MOVE, *march, act* (HANG 行): action toward a position or goal.

NATION (GUO 國): the state; the productive part of an organization; the seat of political power; the entity that controls an ARMY or competitive part of the organization.

OBSTACLES, *barricaded* (XIAN 險): to have barriers; one of the three characteristics of the GROUND; one of six field positions; as a field position, opposite of UNOBSTRUCTED.

OPEN, *meeting, crossing* (JIAO 來): to share the same GROUND without conflict; to come together; a SITUATION that encourages a race; one of nine TERRAINS or STAGES.

OPPORTUNITY: see ADVANTAGE.

OUTMANEUVER (SOU 走): to go astray; to be FORCED into a WEAK POSITION; one of six weaknesses of an army.

OUTSIDE, *external* (WAI 外): not within a TERRITORY or ARMY; one who has a different perspective; one who offers an objective view; opposite of INTERNAL.

PHILOSOPHY, *mission, goals* (TAO 道): the shared GOALS that UNITE an ARMY; a system of thought; a shared viewpoint; literally "the way"; a way to work together; one of the five key factors in ANALYSIS.

PLATEAU (LIU 陸): a type of GROUND without defects; an analogy for any equal, solid, and certain SITUATION; the best place for competition; one of the four types of GROUND.

RESOURCES, *provisions* (LIANG 糧): necessary supplies, most commonly food; one of the five targets of fire attacks.

RESTRAINT: see TIMING.

REWARD, *treasure, money* (BAO 賞): profit; wealth; the necessary compensation for competition; a necessary ingredient for

VICTORY; VICTORY must pay.

SCATTER, *dissipating* (SAN 散): to disperse; to lose UNITY; the pursuit of separate GOALS as opposed to a central MISSION; a situation that causes a FORCE to scatter; one of nine conditions or types of terrain.

SERIOUS, *heavy* (CHONG 重): any task requiring effort and skill; a SITUATION where resources are running low when you are deeply committed to a campaign or heavily invested in a project; a situation where opposition within an organization mounts; one of nine STAGES or types of TERRAIN.

SIEGE (GONG CHENG 攻城): to move against entrenched positions; any movement against an ENEMY'S STRENGTH; literally "strike city"; one of the four forms of attack; the least desirable form of attack.

SITUATION: see GROUND.

SPEED, *hurry* (SAI 馳): to MOVE over GROUND quickly; the ability to ADVANCE POSITIONS in a minimum of time; needed to take advantage of a window of opportunity.

SPREAD-OUT, *wide* (GUANG 廣): a surplus of DISTANCE; one of the six GROUND POSITIONS; opposite of CONSTRICTED.

SPY, *conduit, go-between* (GAAN 間): a source of information; a channel of communication; literally, an "opening between."

STAGE: see GROUND.

STANDARD, *proper, correct* (JANG 正): the expected behavior; the standard approach; proven methods; the opposite of SURPRISE; together with SURPRISE creates MOMENTUM.

STOREHOUSE, *house* (KU 庫): a place where resources are stockpiled; one of the five targets for fire attacks.

STORES, *accumulate, savings* (JI 糧): resources that have been stored; any type of inventory; one of the five targets of fire attacks.

STRENGTH, *fullness, satisfaction* (SAT 實): wealth or abundance or resources; the state of being crowded; the opposite of XU, empty.

SUPPLY WAGONS, *transport* (ZI 輜): the movement of RESOURCES through DISTANCE; one of the five targets of fire attacks.

SUPPORT, *supporting* (ZHII 支): to prop up; to enhance; a GROUND POSITION that you cannot leave without losing STRENGTH; one of six field positions; the opposite extreme of ENTANGLING.

SURPRISE, *unusual, strange* (QI 奇): the unexpected; the innovative; the opposite of STANDARD; together with STANDARDS creates MOMENTUM.

SURROUND: see CONFINED.

SURVIVE, *live, birth* (SHAANG 生): the state of being created, started, or beginning; the state of living or surviving; a temporary condition of fullness; one of five types of spies; the opposite of DEATH.

SYSTEM, *method* (FA 法): a set of procedures; a group of techniques; steps to accomplish a GOAL; one of the five key factors in analysis; the realm of groups who must follow procedures; the opposite of the LEADER.

TERRITORY, *terrain*: see GROUND.

TIMING, *restraint* (JIE 節): to withhold action until the proper time; to release tension; a companion concept to MOMENTUM.

TROOPS: see GROUPS.

UNITY, *whole, oneness* (YI 一): the characteristic of a GROUP that shares a PHILOSOPHY; the lowest number; a GROUP that acts as a unit; the opposite of DIVIDED.

UNOBSTRUCTED, *expert* (TONG 通): without obstacles or barriers; GROUND that allows easy movement; open to new ideas; one of six field positions; opposite of OBSTRUCTED.

VICTORY, *win, winning* (SING 勝): success in an endeavor; getting a reward; serving your mission; an event that produces more than it consumes; to make a profit.

WAR, *competition, army* (BING 兵): a dynamic situation in which POSITIONS can be won or lost; a contest in which a REWARD can be won; the conditions under which the rules of strategy work.

WATER, *river* (SHUI 水): a fast-changing GROUND; fluid CONDITIONS; one of four types of GROUND; an analogy for change.

WEAKNESS, *emptiness, need* (XU 虛): the absence of people or resources; devoid of FORCE; the point of ATTACK for an ADVANTAGE; a characteristic of GROUND that enables SPEED; poor; the opposite of STRENGTH.

WIN, *winning*: see VICTORY.

WIND, *fashion, custom* (FENG 風): the pressure of environmental forces.

Index of Topics in *The Art of War*

This index identifies significant topics, keyed to the chapters, block numbers (big numbers in text), and line numbers (tiny numbers). The format is chapter:block.lines.

About the Authors

Gary Gagliardi

This book's award-winning translator and primary author, Gary Gagliardi, is America's leading authority on Sun Tzu's *The Art of War*. A frequent guest on radio and television talk shows, Gary has written fifteen books on strategy. Ten of his books on Sun Tzu's methods have won award recognition in business, self-help, career, sports, philosophy, multicultural, and youth nonfiction categories.

Gary began studying Sun Tzu's philosophy over thirty years ago. His understanding of strategy was proven in the business world, where his software company became one of the Inc. 500 fastest-growing companies in America and won numerous business awards. After selling his software company, Gary began writing about and teaching Sun Tzu's strategic philosophy full time.

Today he splits his time between Seattle and Las Vegas, living with his wife, Rebecca, and travels extensively for speaking engagements all over the world.

For more see GaryGagliardi.com

garyg@suntzus.com

Shawn R. Frost

Shawn R. Frost has published numerous articles on a variety of topics, and one previous book. He has appeared as an expert guest on many radio and television news programs speaking on the topics of leadership, strategy, education reform and politics.

Shawn first discovered the power of Sun Tzu's *The Art of War* in 1995 at the recommendation of this mentor, Col. Pratt, serving in the U.S. Marine Corps. The book completely altered the direction and quality of his life. After leaving the Marine Corps, Shawn founded a sales corporation that grew quickly using Sun Tzu's principles. After positioning his company for profitable sale, he decided to dedicate himself to deeply understanding Sun Tzu's strategy. In addition to his bachelor's in psychology and minor in Eastern philosophy and MBA in leadership, Shawn began studying with Gary Gagliardi at the Science of Strategy Institute. His past strategy and seminar clients include: Alfred Angelo Bridal, ExxonMobil, and Johnson & Johnson.

Proving that Sun Tzu's rules of competition are universal, in his first effort as a candidate, Shawn unseated a two-term incumbent who was the sitting president of the State School Board Association shocking politicos and the media alike. Using the methods in this book, he has helped other candidates win and selectively works with campaigns as an advisor.

To book Shawn: http://MVPSP.com or http://ShawnFrost.com

Twitter: @StrategyShawn

Want to learn more about Sun Tzu's strategy?

SUNTZUS.COM
SCIENCE OF STRATEGY INSTITUTE

eBooks

Audio books

Audio seminars

Online training

Art of War and Strategy Books By Gary Gagliardi

Sun Tzu's Art of War Playbook in Nine Volumes

Sun Tzu's The Art of War Plus The Art of Sales: Strategy for the Sales Warrior

9 Formulas for Business Success: the Science of Strategy

The Golden Key to Strategy: Everyday Strategy for Everyone

The Art of War Plus The Chinese Revealed

The Art of War Plus The Art of Management: Straegy for Management Warriors

Art of War for Warrior Marketing: Strategy for Conquering Markets

The Art of War Plus The Art of Politics: Strategy for Campaigns (with Shawn Frost)

Making Money By Speaking: The Spokesperson Strategy

The Warrior Class: 306 Lessons in Strategy

The Art of War for the Business Warrior: Strategy for Entrepreneurs

The Art of War Plus The Warrior's Apprentice: Strategy for Teens

The Art of War Plus Strategy for Sales Managers: Strategy for Sales Groups

The Ancient Bing-fa: Martial Arts Strategy

Strategy Against Terror: Ancient Wisdom for Today's War

The Art of War Plus The Art of Career Building: Strategy for Promotion

Sun Tzu's Art of War Plus Parenting Teens

The Art of War Plus Its Amazing Secrets: The Keys to Ancient Chinese Science

Art of War Plus Art of Love: Strategy for Romance

37720389R00127

Made in the USA
Middletown, DE
04 December 2016